Mental Health, Psychotherapy and Judaism

Seymour Hoffman, Ph. D.

Mental Health, Psychotherapy and Judaism

Seymour Hoffman, Ph. D.

GOLDEN SKY

Golden Sky
New York

Golden Sky is an imprint of *Mondial*.

Seymour Hoffman, Ph. D.:

Mental Health, Psychotherapy and Judaism

© 2011 Seymour Hoffman

This book or parts thereof may not be reproduced in any form, stored in a retrieval system, or transmitted in any form by any means — electronic, mechanical, photocopy, recording, or otherwise — without the prior written permission of the publisher or the author, except as provided by United States of America copyright law.

Cover: © Golden Sky

ISBN: 978-1-59569-221-4

Library of Congress Control Number: 2011934329

www.goldenskybooks.com

Table of Contents

Introduction and Dedication i
Foreword iii
Preface v

1. First Mental Health Clinic Under Ultra-Orthodox Auspices 1
2. Behavior Change via Cognitive Change: Rabbinic Views 15
3. "The Ends Justify the Means": Rabbinic Strategic Interventions 21
4. "Kosher" Talebearing: A Modest Proposal 31
5. "Helpmate Unto Him": Dialectical Cotherapy 39
6. Rabbis and Psychologists: "And They Both Walked Together"? 53
7. Brief Rabbinic Interventions in Psychological Treatment 63
8. Religious Issues in Psychological Treatment: Contemporary Responsa 77

Addenda:

9. "Therapist Friendly" and "Therapist Unfriendly" Views of Psychotherapy 93
10. Ultra-Orthodox Rabbinic Responses to Religious Obsessive-Compulsive Disorder 103

Acknowledgements 127

Introduction and Dedication

For too many years there was a distinct chasm between therapists and rabbis, as each buttressed themselves behind their profession's truths and disparaging goals.

In the past two decades this has changed with an enhanced regard and understanding of the influence of that common element of human nature, loosely referred to as spiritualism. People in the helping professions as well as in the general public give credit to the interaction and influence of this vaguely understood aspect of humanity, whereas rabbis and theologians have come to appreciate the skills and experience of community workers in the field of mental health and family care.

Nefesh Israel is an organization of observant clinicians which recognize the advantages of pulling together with men of the spirit, pooling resources and giving scope for members of both fields to cooperate, enrich each other, even while recognizing the differences in their orientation, purpose and methods.

Dr. Hoffman's efforts in this book are a fine example of how this cross-pollination is put into effect on a day to day basis. The subjects are both practical and enlightening, demonstrating through many case histories and analysis, how the religious authorities and the mental health professionals-psychologists, psychiatrists, social workers and therapists, can work for mutual benefits. However, the difficulties still existing, the prejudices and pre-conceptions that remain in certain circles towards clinician, are also given exposure.

Nefesh Israel is proud to sponsor "Mental Health, Psychotherapy and Judaism", our fourth publication and the first in English. (The contents of this book do not necessarily reflect the views of Nefesh Israel). This book is affectionately dedicated to Dr. Judy Guedalia, co-founder and co-chairperson of Nefesh Israel.

Dr. Guedalia, or Judi as everyone calls her affectionately, is never boring. She can, in fact, be outrageous, hilarious, or irreverent, but underneath it all there's a warm Jewish heart and a polished and skilled professional, which keeps her and Nefesh Israel on the right track. Judi has made her mark in her field of neuropsychiatry; she has been exceedingly capable in diagnosing and treating more patients that she cares to remember. She has won the respect of her colleagues and readers of her articles in professional journals as well as in the more popular papers where her case studies appear regularly. Her pioneering work with terror victims is only one example of her breakthrough work.

Judi has never been afraid to take a strong stand when she found injustice, abuse or charlatans whether among ordinary citizens or professional and/or religious leaders. Nefesh Israel has been at the forefront, due to her concern and conscience, in bringing to light and combating misdemeanors of every sort. The backlash Judi has personally absorbed from such forthrightness, has not been easy, but then Judi is not easily thwarted.

When Judi got sick the hundreds of prayers and tehillim which rent the heavens on her behalf from all over the world surely must have made a difference. We all continue to entreat HaKadosh Baruch Hu to continue to shine His countenance on her, on Nefesh Israel which she co-founded and nurtured and on Klal Yisrael.

Leah Abramowitz, M.S.W., Co-chair of Nefesh Israel and Director, Geriatric Institute at Shaare Zedek Medical Center.

Foreword

Psychotherapy and Judaism have an important relationship and also an extended historical connection. The headquarters for Judaism's understanding of the importance of psychotherapy was originally stated by King Solomon in Proverbs chapter 12, verse 25: "If there is anxiety in the heart of man *'yashchena'* and thereby turn it into joy through a good *"davar."*

The Babylonian Talmud in three separate places, Yuma, 75a, Sotah, 42b and Sanhedrin, 100a, cites the verse from Proverbs and discusses the meaning of *"yashchena."* The Talmud states that a disagreement exists between Rav Ammi and Rav Assi. One rabbi states "you should force it out of your mind." The other rabbi states "you should talk with others about it." It appears they are presenting entirely different approaches to dealing with emotional difficulties. One recommends forgetting about it and pushing it away, while the other appears to recommend doing the opposite — sharing it with someone else by speaking about it. However, if we interpret their disagreement according to present day psychological knowledge and understanding, we may interpret their opinions in a different light. It appears to me that actually they are in agreement that psychotherapy is important to alleviate anxiety and stress. What they are disagreeing about is the preferable method of treatment. The rabbi who states "forcing it out of your mind "(cognition) is actually recommending using cognitive restructuring, and behavioral and strategic approaches.The other rabbi recommends specific "talking therapy" with psychodynamic understanding. This interpretation is corroborated in the second part of the verse in Proverbs by the use of the word *"davar." "Davar"* can mean a "thing", like a procedure in cognitive or behavioral therapy, or strategic therapeutic actions to effect change. It can also mean from the same root, *"d-v-r"*, talking -allowing the person to talk out his problems and understand his unconscious motivation. With the appropriate timely interpretation this brings joy. The person is now able to have greater ability to effect positive change in his or her emotional conflicts that are causing stress. He or she has the ability to be more flexible and open in making choices to improve intrapersonal and interpersonal life. That joy is sometimes called the "Aha phenomenon" as in "Now, I really understand." The individual has internalized the cause of his distress and can now choose to act differently.

Research in all the mental health disciplines has shown that people go to their religious leader first when individual or family problems develop. It is therefore incumbent in Judaism upon the rabbi to be well-trained in mental health issues so that he can differentiate issues that he can help with and those where a referral to a professional is necessary. Mental health practitioners need to turn to rabbis who understand emotional disorders when they need halachic guidance. The increased cooperation between rabbis and mental health professionals is a desideratum. Cooperation and collaboration between rabbis and therapists is one of the important issues discussed in articles that Dr. Hoffman has offered us in his valuable book.

In my opinion, there is no specific Jewish psychology or psychiatric treatment protocol, just as there is no specific Jewish way to treat pneumonia, or to surgically remove a gall bladder. However, the Bible, Talmud, *Chazal* and later rabbinic commentaries had great insights into human nature, drives, desires and coping mechanisms. Examples of such insights are documented by the author of this book and by Greenberg and Shefler in their interesting and informative article.

I believe that mental health professionals, psychotherapists and clergymen, as well as those interested in the interface between mental health and Judaism will find this slim volume a pleasant and worthwhile read.

Joshua H. Werblowsky, M.D., D-L.F.A.P.A.
Clinical Associate Professor of Psychiatry, Drexel University College of Medicine and Lecturer, Schlesinger Jewish Medical Ethics Institute.

Preface

Religion (halacha) and Mental Health (Psychotherapy) share a common concern and goal — the quality of life and its improvement and enrichment. Religion provides man with a purpose, direction, ethical and moral rules and values to make his life more meaningful and worthwhile. Psychotherapy's purpose and function is first, to give the troubled person relief from suffering, to ease his psychic pain, and then to equip him better to live in peace, affection and stable equilibrium with himself, his immediate objects and the world around him.

However, there are basic differences between the two disciplines. While psychotherapy is anthropocentric, religion is theocentric. While the former's goal and measuring rod is man's psychological well-being (however defined by the mental health expert), the latter's goal and measuring rod is man's ethical behavior and obedience to the will of God. Halacha (Jewish Law) does not recognize man's rights but the duties of man to God. Religious values therefore, may at times differ and be incongruent with the values held by mental health professionals. Behavior that may be unacceptable from a religious perspective may be acceptable, if not preferable, from a mental health perspective.

Professor Kate Lowenthal, (2006) in a comprehensive and informative article entitled, "Orthodox Judaism: Features and Issues for Psychotherapy", makes several cogent and relevant points:

1. The ultra-orthodox community and their rabbis have been negative about using mainstream psychotherapy and counseling services. Jewish tradition has always endorsed the obligation to seek medical treatment, and the doctor is empowered by G-d to heal. Medical treatment for psychosis – particularly medication

– is seen as appropriate. For the "minor" disorders (depression, anxiety), and for social problems, there are reservations among orthodox Jewish authorities regarding seeking counseling and psychotherapy.

2. There are several areas in which the values of Orthodox Judaism may conflict – or appear to conflict – with the needs of psychotherapeutic work. These conflicts and apparent conflicts are primary reasons for the reluctance of many orthodox rabbis to endorse unconditionally the use of counseling and psychotherapy. Orthodox counselors and therapists will have received training and guidance in dealing with these issues, and will liaise closely with the rabbinate in their day-to-day work, so their work is usually endorsed by the rabbinate.

3. Jewish law does not condone homosexuality, masturbation, extra-marital or pre-marital sexual relations. Thus any indication that these practices can be condoned or supported is not appropriate for orthodox Jews, even though of course all these practices can and do happen. Therapists who do not share orthodox Jewish values and beliefs may think or suggest that an orthodox Jewish client is being made guilty or anxious as a result of religious prohibitions about sexual behavior. Appropriate therapeutic support can only be given by a therapist who understands that the religious prohibitions are givens, and the feelings and conflicts of clients must be dealt within the context of the clients' probable acceptance that the laws about sexual behavior are right, even if s/he does not find them easy or convenient.

4. Marriage is regarded as a holy and desirable state, and every attempt to preserve a marriage is regarded as praiseworthy and religiously meritorious. Nevertheless, there is no rabbinic support for domestic violence or other forms of abuse. Again it is important for therapists to be aware of the complex issues in religious law, and to have appropriate rabbinic contacts.

5. There are assertions that obsessive-compulsive disorder (OCD) is more common among orthodox Jews than in other groups, but there is no reliable prevalence work, and Lewis (1998) has concluded that while obsessionality as a personality trait is more likely among the religious, probably as a result of the religious valuing scrupulosity, OCD as a psychiatric disorder is not more likely in any of the religious groups studied, compared to the general population. Greenberg & Witztum (1994) concluded that religion can provide the framework for the expression of OCD symptoms, but is unlikely to be a direct cause.

It seems most judicious that rabbis should consult and refer religious patients to mental health practitioners who are religious or at least are sufficiently knowledgeable of Jewish law and customs and respect the values of their patients, and that the latter should consult with and refer their clients to rabbis who have a basic knowledge and understanding of psychopathology and psychotherapy, when there is a need for halachic guidance.

* * *

This slim volume focuses on the interface between psychotherapy and Judaism. The topics considered are varied and relate to theoretical as well as practical issues. Reports of effective therapeutic treatments involving rabbis and psychologist, markedly differing opinions of various rabbinic authorities regarding psychotherapy, examples of psychological wisdom and insights of rabbis and religious leaders in effecting change in people, description of the workings of a unique mental health clinic under ultra-orthodox auspices, and responsa of contemporary rabbis to psychotherapy-halachic questions and issues, are some of the topics discussed in this volume.

In the addenda, examples of "Therapist-Friendly" and "Therapist-Unfriendly" views and comments of prominent rabbinic figures are presented as well as the clearly articulated views of a prominent orthodox Jewish psychiatrist and psychoanalyst, on the relationship between Torah and psychotherapy.

The last article, by two prominent Israeli mental health practitioners and authors, discusses the views and responses of two psychologically sophisticated, insightful and revered haredi rabbis to ultra-orthodox people suffering from religious symptoms of obsessive-compulsive disorder.

It is hoped that rabbis, therapists, mental health practitioners, as well as those interested in the interface between psychotherapy and Judaism, will find interest and benefit from reading this book.

References

Greenberg, D. & Witztum, E. (1994) The influence of cultural factors on obsessive compulsive disorders: Religious symptoms in a religious society. *Israel Journal of Psychiatry and Related Sciences*, 31, 211-220.

Lewis, C.A. (1998) Cleanliness is next to G-dliness: Religiosity and obsessiveness. *Journal of Religion and Health*, 37, 49-61.

Loewenthal, K M (2006) *Orthodox Judaism: Features and Issues for Psychotherapy.* In: The Psychologies in Religion. Springer Publishing, UK.

1

*First Mental Health Clinic
Under Ultra-Orthodox Auspices*

Haredi ("one who is in awe of G-d") is the most theological conservative form of orthodox Judaism. Haredi (ultra-orthodox) life is very family-centered and families tend to be large, reflecting adherence to the Torah commandment "be fruitful and multiply" (Genesis,1:28, 9:1,7). Depending on various factors, boys and girls attend separate schools and proceed to higher religious study in a yeshiva (orthodox Jewish institute of learning) or seminary respectively, starting anywhere between the ages of 13 and 18. A significant proportion of young men remain in yeshiva until their marriage often arranged through facilitated dating. Many also continue to study Torah in an institute for married men for many years after marriage. In many haredi communities, studying in secular institutions is discouraged, although some have educational facilities for vocational training or run professional programs for men and women. Television, films, reading secular newspapers and magazines and using the internet for non-business purposes are forbidden.

Many haredim view manner of dress as an important way to ensure Jewish identity and distinctiveness. In addition, a simple, understated mode of dress is seen as conducive to inner reflection and spiritual growth. As such, many haredim are wary of modern clothing (some of which may compromise their standards of modesty). Many men have beards, most dress in dark suits, and wear a wide-brimmed black hat and wear a skullcap at all times. Women adhere to meticulous modesty standards, and hence wear long skirts and long sleeves, high necklines and some form of head covering or wig after marriage.

Haredi Judaism advocates segregation from non-Jewish culture, although not from non-Jewish society entirely. It is characterized by its focus on community-wide Torah study. Engaging in the commercial world is often seen as a legitimate means to achieving a livelihood, but participation in modern society is not perceived as an inherently worthy ambition.

* * *

The ultra-orthodox community and their rabbis have been negative about using mainstream psychotherapy and counseling services. Spitzer (2003) regards it as essential that orthodox and Hasidic patients with psychiatric and psychological disturbances are seen only by professionals from a similar cultural background. Spitzer and others argue that the behavior and feelings of orthodox patients cannot be understood by others, and appropriate help and treatment can only be developed by those with a full immersion in the cultural and religious values and practices of the community.

The mental health facilities where we are employed are under ultra-orthodox auspices and the administrative and professional staff is comprised of haredi/religious employees. The facilities provide free psychiatric and psychological services to the haredi community and take into consideration the special religious needs and requirements of their clients. As expected, the staff is required to dress in modest attire and separate waiting rooms are appropriated for men and women where one can find religious books and religious reading material. In the staff meetings, male and female members sit at opposite sides of the room and in different parts of the dining room at lunch time.

Since receiving psychiatric and psychological treatment is generally viewed by the haredi community as a stigma, the clinic is called a community clinic and not a mental health clinic. It provides psychiatric (medication) and psychological (psychotherapy) treatment as well as social services to adults and children and a separate day treatment program for men and women. Psychotherapy includes individual, couple, family and group therapy. Because of halachic (Jewish law) considerations, separate treatment groups are held for women and for men. However, an exception was made when a highly respected arbiter was convinced by the co-leader of a parents' group of schizophrenic children that the presence of both parents in these group meetings was essential and gave his permission to permit both parents of the children to participate in the group meetings with the proviso that they were over the age of forty-five, refrained from discussing intimate matters and that there was no mixed gender seating.

The clinic arranged five highly successful and relevant bi-monthly lectures to which the staff and other mental health practitioners treating religious clientele participated. The presenters, experts in their field, discussed a variety of topics relevant to the haredi community, which stimulated a great deal of interest and discussion. The topics included: 1. Issues and problems in treating haredi patients; 2. Group therapy for haredi/religious pedophiles; 3. Treatment of sexually abused survivors; 4. Eating disorders in the haredi community; 5. Treatment of religious patients with Same Sex Attraction

* * *

The Day Hospital Treatment Center provides a facility for more seriously disturbed patients who require more intense treatment than the clinic can provide. The patients spend five hours a day at the center, five days a week, and receive individual and group therapy, psychopharmacological treatment and adjunctive therapies. They also receive free breakfasts and lunches. The male patients can participate in religious services and attend lectures that are delivered by volunteers. Receiving psychiatric and psychological care in this supportive and caring environment, which is consistent with their religious values and life styles, frequently prevents psychiatric hospitalization. A psychiatric inpatient facility is presently being built to serve patients who require hospital care.

* * *

Although the haredi community has become in recent years more open to seeking mental-health treatment in times of need, there still remains much stigmatism regarding mental disorders, especially when one enters the "shiduchim" (marriage arrangement) phase of life. Though there exists a tendency in religious and even secular communities a general inclination to direct young men and women who suffer from physical defects and/or psychiatric disorders not to disclose them, this tendency is very prevalent in the haredi community. Revealing their personal defects and disorders before the marriage may result in a drastic decrease in the number and quality of "offers" they receive. Young haredi men and women in the "shiduchim phase" come for treatment in a state of great distress as they are concerned what will happen after they get married and their "terrible secret" becomes known. Treatment in such cases is very difficult because revealing the "secret" before marriage and thereby enabling the patient to lessen his/her anxiety, is frequently not a viable option.

To illustrate the above dilemma, two cases that were brought to supervision are presented below:

A 23 year old haredi student who recently got engaged sought psychological treatment so that "he will be able to discontinue taking psychiatric medication before his marriage" that was scheduled to take place in several weeks. His rabbi cautioned him not to reveal to his fiancée that he was receiving psychiatric and psychological treatment and dismissed several of his concerns and reservations regarding marrying his intended as insignificant.* Unbeknownst to him, his

---

* In contrast to the attitude and behavior of the rabbi referred to above, Rabbi, Dr. Abraham Twerski, a prominent Torah scholar and psychiatrist, wrote in the ultra-orthodox magazine "Hamodia" (January 29, 2009) a response to a woman who sought his advice after finding herself in a similar situation as the young husband mentioned above:
"I have repeatedly pleaded with people not to withhold important information precisely because of situations like this. Your husband's parents felt that if they revealed that he was taking medication, that would ruin his

fiancée was also being treated at the clinic which he discovered two weeks prior to the wedding when he saw her entering the clinic. He requested from his therapist to provide him information whether his betrothed was a patient at the clinic and what was her psychiatric problem. The therapist explained to him that he was not at liberty to provide him this information because of professional ethics and suggested that he "come clean" with her regarding his psychiatric condition, inform her that he saw her at the clinic and request her to "come clean" with him, in order that they can begin their marriage on the "right foot"-openness, honesty and trust between them. Unfortunately, the patient did not act on his therapist's suggestion and a month later, the couple separated.

A young haredi, single woman sought psychological treatment for anxiety and panic attacks. Her anxiety was exacerbated by her relentless concern and worry regarding how her husband to be will react to her psychological symptoms. It was clear to her that if she wanted to marry a suitable haredi man, she was obligated to hide the fact that she suffered from these psychological problems and that she was in psychological treatment. As her haredi therapist explained to me in supervision, 'When one meets a prospective candidate for marriage for the allotted five meetings, one is obligated to 'wear a mask', if one wishes to get married."

The therapist found herself in a quandary-on the one hand she believed that being secretive, deceitful and untrusting with one's intended is highly destructive and a poor formula and basis for a successful and lasting marriage; on the other hand, in the haredi community, there is the unfortunate reality that being open and forthright will sabotage any possibility for the patient to find and marry an appropriate mate. When the patient mentioned to her therapist that she met with a man several times and both seemed

---

chances of finding a wife, so they withheld the information "for his sake." But did they help him despite their intentions? Parents! I plead to you. Have pity on your children. Do not cause them suffering by withholding information. As you see it can cause them misery rather than happiness."

interested in marriage, the therapist decided to encourage the patient to "come out of the closet" and inform him of her situation since her many positive qualities will outweigh her minor defects. This way she would be able to set aside her intense fears and anxieties and begin her marriage in a positive way. The patient, after considerable hesitation and deliberation, agreed and discussed with her therapist how to reveal her secret in the most effective manner. The patient was also informed by the therapist that she was available to meet with the both of them if they requested a meeting. In the following meeting, the patient reported that her suitor was appreciative that she informed him that she was receiving psychological help for her anxiety and panic attacks and scheduled to meet her the following week.

A frequent complaint of the female patients is of being overwhelmed with the burdens of running the household and being depressed. Upon further probing, they speak about serious marital discord and alienation that has been going on for many years and feelings of impotence to change the situation. Many complain about the absence of the husband to help in household chores and in taking care of the children. In spite of serious marital difficulties in the beginning of their marriage, many of these women continue to have more children. One of the women when asked why she continued to have more children after they were having serious marital problems responded that, "it was not respectable to have few children." A considerable amount of women (and men) attend the clinic without the knowledge of their spouse for fear that they would object to their coming or that this information may be used against them in the future, which places stumbling blocks at attempts for possible reconciliation and rehabilitation of strife-ridden marriages.

* * *

Other frequent symptoms that bring haredi men and women to the clinic are obsessional fears, thoughts and preoccupation regarding religious rituals and behavior and compulsive behavior on their part to deal with it. Generally the religious content concerns issues related to cleanliness related to prayer and tasks involving ritual immersion, separation of meat and milk products and utensils, and various aspects of prayer. Frequently these symptoms require the close cooperation of religious authorities (Huppert, Siev, and Kushner, 2007; Greenberg and Shefler, 2008), and at times, their direct intervention. (Slanger, 1996).

Below are presented two brief vignettes of the brief interventions of rabbis in the treatment of OCD with religious content. (Greenberg and Shefler, 2008)

> A woman was very concerned that she found signs of the cross wherever she walked, in the pavement, the window frames, etc., and that as a religious Jewish person she should avoid these signs of Christianity. She went to see her rabbi, renowned for his saintliness and understanding of mental health issues, and described her difficulties. In response, as she sat before him, he put one index finger across the other to form the shape of a cross, raised it to his lips and kissed the shape. His non-verbal response was to make it clear that there is a distinction between a religious symbol and everyday objects, and she was not to seek such symbols where they did not exist. His message was made even more powerful, as he was modeling "kissing the cross" to show that such everyday objects need cause no alarm and should be confronted.

> A young man had approached his rabbi about his repetitions in prayer. His rituals of repetition concerned the most important section of the daily prayers, the Shema (declaration of the unity of the Creator). His rabbi's reply was that he was to stop saying all three paragraphs of the Shema completely for two weeks. He returned to the rabbi after two weeks, and was now told to restore the third paragraph alone, with no repetitions.

He returned two weeks later and the second paragraph was restored, the next visit all was restored except the first and most important sentence, the Shema. Finally, he was told to restore the Shema but to be careful not to repeat any parts of the prayer. For eight weeks this young man had left out the most important line of his daily prayers.

"The role of the rabbi differs from that of a therapist in several ways. The rabbi is an expert in Jewish law and has the authority to make decisions on religious matters. The therapist, on the other hand, is an expert on OCD. He may have status but not authority over the patient, whom he advises." (Greenberg and Shefler, 2008).

* * *

It goes without saying that all decisions that are made in references to the patients that have religious ramifications, pass through a "halachic prism" before being acted upon.

To illustrate the above: The professional staff of the clinic and the educational staff at the girl's school, decided after many deliberations, that a 10 year old girl should be removed from her home because of the detrimental effect the parents were having on her, and be placed in a foster home. However, before implementing this decision, a recognized halachic authority was consulted, and after meeting with the staff, ruled that it was preferable that the child remain in her home and continue to receive psychological treatment rather than break up a Jewish family. The staff accepted the rabbi's decision and arranged for the child and parents to continue to receive psychological treatment at the clinic.

* * *

Below are two interesting anecdotal examples of the influence of halachic considerations in the implementation of psychological treatment.

A young haredi clinical psychology intern reported in supervision that she was seeing a middle-aged mother of four who was constantly being plagued by obsessional fears and thoughts that "her husband would die," "her son would be run over by a car," etc., which were seriously impeding her daily functioning. Even mentioning these thoughts increased her anxieties and fears since she feared that her utterances may cause it to happen. After considerable deliberations, the supervisor suggested a behavioral intervention ("habituation")-that she request the patient to verbalize aloud her fearful thoughts in the treatment room and tape-record them and listen to them at home twice a day. The supervisee, however, raised an halachic issue: By prescribing this intervention technique, she and the patient will be going against the rabbinic caveat/prohibition, "A person must never open his mouth to Satan," and "Contract is made to the lips" (ie., one should be cautious what he emits from his mouth, as speech has power and influence and may cause the feared event to eventuate.) Since the supervisee was hesitant in executing a therapeutic intervention which may possibly compromise the religious values of the therapist and her patient, the supervisor felt obligated to raise this issue with a rabbi who permitted this intervention since the goal was to enable the patient to extricate herself from her oppressive symptoms.

A young religious clinical psychology intern raised an interesting ethical/religious dilemma in supervision. A haredi young man confided to her that he is a homosexual, has had relationships in the past with men and is presently waiting for his mother to arrange a "shidduch" for him. His reason for wanting to get married was to please his mother with whom he has a strong symbiotic relationship, and who is pressuring him to get married and who is unaware of his sexual proclivities. The therapist had made many attempts to dissuade the patient from following this course with little success. The therapist raised the question whether she is obligated to inform the mother and his prospective intended about his sexual proclivities and orientation since there is a biblical prohibition, "Thou shall not stand idly by the blood of thy neighbor" (Leviticus, 19, 16), which is interpreted by the rabbis as an obligation to attempt to save and protect one's neighbor's life, possessions and emotional and spiritual wellbeing.

After consulting with a rabbinic authority, the supervisor informed his supervisee that she is not obligated to inform the patient's mother and intended since a psychologist differs from a layman in that he is professionally obligated to keep confidential material and risks causing damage to his status, income, the therapeutic relationship and is also liable to possible imprisonment, if he betrays the confidence of his clients. He suggested that the therapist inform her patient that he plans to schedule a family meeting and inform his parents that she has strong doubts and reservations that their son is emotionally and psychologically ready and capable, at this time, to marry and assume the responsibility of being a husband and father, and that she was very concerned about the possible damage that will result by this action to him, his intended and future children.

Conclusions

A recent study by Professor Eliezer Schnall of Yeshiva University and colleagues (2010) concluded that the mental health needs of the Orthodox community are not being sufficiently addressed and the service gaps are particularly pronounced in the haredi Orthodox and Chasidic communities. Schnall called the results a "wake-up call," and said there is still a stigma in the Orthodox community attached to mental illness that prevents people from seeking help. An additional factor impeding good mental health services is their cost, he said.

The study showed that the most common problem for which Orthodox Jews seek mental health services is marital difficulties. More services for children and teenagers are needed, and there is a lack of services for substance abuse problems, the report found. Most respondents in the study said few of their patients were referred by their rabbis. Researchers said this indicates the need to train Orthodox rabbis to recognize mental illness and understand that proper treatment can help.

The establishment of a clinic under ultra-orthodox sponsorship is a bold and pioneering step that should be applauded, as it facilitates and encourages members of the haredi community that are in need of psychiatric and psychological treatment to obtain help in a "religious-friendly" environment where their religious values and customs are respected and accommodated. In addition, it enables ultra-orthodox psychology interns and other haredi mental health workers to train and gain clinical experience in an environment that is consistent with their value system and way of life.* Establishment of more mental health clinics under haredi auspices should be encouraged.

---

* In regard to this, see Garr, M. and Marans, G. (2001) Ultra-orthodox women in Israel: A pilot study project in social work education, Social Work Education, vol. 2, Issue 4.

References

Greenberg, D. and Shefler, G. (2008) Ultra-orthodox rabbinic responses to religious obsessive-compulsive disorder. Israel Journal of Psychiatry and Related Sciences, 3, 4, 183-192.

Huppert, D. H., Siev, J. and Kushner, E. S. (2007) When religion and obsessive-compulsive disorder collide: Treating scrupulosity in ultra-orthodox Jews, Journal of clinical psychology, 63, 10, 925-941.

Schnall, E., Feinberg, S., Feinberg, K., & Kalkstein, S. (2010, August). Psychological disorder and stigma: A 25-year follow-up study in the Orthodox Jewish community. The 118th Annual Convention of the American Psychological Association, San Diego, CA.

Slanger, C., (1996) Orthodox rabbinic attitudes to mental health professionals and referral patterns. Tradition, 31, 1, 22-33.

Spitzer, J. (2003) Caring for Jewish Patients. Abingdon, Oxford: Radcliffe Medical Press.

2

*Behavior Change
Via Cognitive Change:
Rabbinic Views*

The issue of what causes behavior change in people has been debated for decades. The psychoanalytically oriented practitioners and theoreticians insist that insight is a prerequisite to real change and that change without insight is an illusion. On the other hand, the nondynamic cognitive-behavioral and strategic therapists argue that enduring behavior and attitude changes are made more likely by first getting a person to engage in new behavior. Insight, in their view, is frequently a by-product, rather than a cause of change.

"Many people who are depressed believe that they "just need to become motivated" but the very symptoms often block such motivation. Therefore, if the person waits to become motivated they wait in vain. Ironically, engaging in an activity even when you feel unmotivated to do so can lead to feeling motivated. We call this working from the outside-in."[1]

The latter view seems to be consistent with that of the author of *Sefer Ha'Ḥinukh*, who in explicating the 613 Commandments makes the point many times that "one's heart is influenced by one's actions."

Similar views are found in the Talmud. "Rabbi Judah said, 'Man should always occupy himself with learning Torah and its Commandments, even for ulterior motives, for eventually he will do it for idealistic reasons'."[2]

In his commentary to the *Ethics of the Fathers* Maimonides[3] recommends that a person who wishes to dispense a large sum of money

---

1. CR Martelle, ME Addis and NS Jacobson, *Depression in Context* (New York: W.W. Norton, 2001).
2. Talmud Nazir, 23b.
3. Mishna Avot, 3:15.

for charity should dispense it in small amounts rather than in one large sum, in order that the trait of generosity become instilled in him or her.

(Likewise, Milgram points out in his classic study on obedience that prohibited and evil behavior, when repeated, tends to become the norm. "Once the individual has begun to do evil, he continues doing evil, rather than say to himself, 'Everything I have done to this point is bad and now I acknowledge it by breaking it off'."[4]

The Talmud says, "If a person transgresses a prohibition and repeats it, it becomes to him as if it was permissible."[5]

The concepts of cognitive transformation and cognitive dissonance were also used by the rabbis in understanding and modifying human behavior. Ibn Ezra, in discussing the Tenth Commandment, "Thou shalt not covet...your neighbor's wife" states:

Many people will be puzzled by this command. Is it conceivable that there should exist a man who does not, at some time or another, covet a beautiful object? Let me now give you a parable. A country yokel in his right senses will not covet a beautiful princess, since he knows it is impossible to possess her, just the same as he will not seriously desire to have wings like a bird. For this reason the thinking person will neither desire nor covet. Since he knows that the Almighty has forbidden him his neighbor's wife, such a course of action will be even further from his mind than from that of the country yokel in regard to the princess.[6]

By viewing his neighbor's wife as even more inaccessible than a princess (cognitive transformation) man can control his desires and train himself not to covet.

---

4. M Milgram. Obedience to Authority: An Experimental View (New York: Harper & Row, 1974).

5. Talmud Yoma, 86b.

6. Ibn Ezra, on Exodus, 20:14.

In the Tractate Avodah Zara,[7] it is recorded that when Rabbi Akiva saw the beautiful wife of the wicked Tornosrophus, he spat, laughed and cried. The Talmud explains that the reason that Rabbi Akiva spat was that he was repulsed by the thought that she came from a putrid drop of semen. By focusing on this thought, Rabbi Akiva was able to negate, nullify and counter his illicit and unacceptable feelings thoughts and impulses.

In Avot of Rabbi Natan, chapter 16, it is related that one night, the governmental authorities sent two women to seduce Rabbi Akiva, and he said that he thought of the detestable things that they ate in order to distance himself from them. By focusing on the abovementioned negative thoughts and images, Rabbi Akiva was able to negate, nullify and counter any illicit and unacceptable feelings, thoughts and impulses.

Cognitive dissonance is a state in which a discrepancy exists between perception and expectation or precepts and concepts.[8] This situation motivates cognitive processes and defense mechanisms. There exists a strong human drive to reduce dissonance and resolve internal conflict by changing one's view or behavior to conform with one's statements and actions.

Examples of cognitive dissonance are found in the rabbinic literature. In Genesis Rabba[9] Joseph's behavior toward his brothers is discussed:

Simon incited his brothers against Joseph and also threw him in a pit. Since Joseph wanted to uproot the hatred and resentment he felt toward Simon, he [Joseph] catered to all his [Simon's] physical needs by providing him with food and drink, and he bathed and applied ointment to his body.

---

7. Talmud Avodah Zara, 20a.
8. L Festinger, A Theory of Cognitive Dissonance (Evanston, IL: Row, Peterson & Co., 1957).
9. Genesis Raba, 91:8.

The rabbis comment that "An action retrains behavior and thought. A thought does not retrain behavior or thought."[10] If one really wants to uproot an evil thought or feeling toward another, he has to do a benevolent act.

The Talmud sages ruled that if one is presented with a situation in which at the same moment a friend's animal is lying under its burden and an enemy needs help in loading his animal, one is obligated to first aid the latter, in order to subjugate the evil impulse.[11] Removing hatred from one's heart is a greater deed than relieving the suffering of an animal. By creating cognitive dissonance between negative feeling (hatred) and positive action (providing service) one is forced to change one's feelings to conform to one's behavior.

Another example of the above is the story about Rabbi Israel Lipkin (Salanter), founder and spiritual father of the "Musar" movement, who while riding in a train, was treated in a disrespectful and abusive manner by a fellow passenger. Upon learning later on that the object of his abuse was the revered Rabbi Lipkin, the young man apologized profusely and asked the rabbi for his forgiveness. Rabbi Lipkin informed him that he forgave him immediately and then proceeded to help him in various ways. When asked by his bewildered disciples why he displayed such kindness to a person who previously insulted and abused him, the rabbi explained that he wasn't sure that he totally forgave the young man, and by helping him, he was able to rid any remnants of anger and resentment towards him.

Jewish religious leaders, moralists, and commentators have always been acute observers of humanity. An analysis of their recommended techniques for interpersonal behavior, self-control, and behavior change may well be a practical contribution to contemporary psychology and psychotherapy.[12]

---

10. Talmud Kiddushin, 59b.
11. Talmud Bava Metsia, 32b.
12. S Schimmel, "Free-will, Guilt and Self-control in Rabbinic Judaism" in Judaism and Contemporary Psychology 26, no. 4 (1977): 418-29.

3

The Ends Justify the Means:
Rabbinic Strategic Interventions

Strategic therapy is a direct treatment approach that aims to relieve symptoms, resolve conflicts, and free people from their neurotic morass in the shortest time possible. This approach relies heavily on manipulation to effect change quickly and effectively. Manipulation in the most concrete sense is the act of controlling with the hands or the mind. The use of manipulation has produced wide debate and heated reaction among psychotherapists of all persuasions. On the one hand, there are those who decry its use because they think it is patronizing, infantilizing, presumptuous, coercive, deceptive, abusively authoritarian, unethical, inconsistent with respect for the client and incompatible with developing a trusting therapeutic relationship.

On the other hand, there are therapists who argue that "life is one big manipulation" and insist that it is involved in all forms of therapy, ranging from analytically orientated to behavioral and strategic, though it may not be equally obvious in all forms. In their view, manipulation is nothing more than influence, and in therapy, "one cannot not influence" just as "one cannot not communicate". The question is not whether to influence or not but how to do it in the most constructive, humane, non-exploitative, effective, and expeditious manner, in order to effect positive change in the client and help him ameliorate his symptoms and resolve his conflicts. Manipulation in its most benign and simple form is no more complicated than a mother placing a band-aid or a kiss on the wound of a child to "make it all better." In its more complex form, manipulation involves deception and shrewd, devious, and strategic interventions.

The dialectical cotherapy approach (Hoffman, et. al., 1994) has been criticized on moral grounds. "It is difficult to accept a method of therapy based on deliberate dishonesty. It is hard to believe that the deception has no long-term ill effects. Even if it succeeds, does the end justify the means?" (Chazan, 2000)

According to this view, treatment approaches that make use of placebos and paradoxical interventions popularized by such prominent strategic therapists as Haley, Madanes, Frankl, Zeig, Lankton, and Milton Erickson, to name a few, would be considered unethical and unacceptable. The paradoxical approach involves deceiving the client, as the therapist suggests a certain behavior but expects that the client will do the opposite, in view of his resistance. Doherty and Boss (1991), state that, "If paradoxical methods are used in a way that invades the autonomy of clients, deceives the client, or undermines the therapist's trustworthiness, then they are unethical. Haley (1976), argues, "If it is essential for the cure that deceit be used, it might be justified on that basis." There are those who claim that the paradoxical approach does not negate the approach that respects autonomy if it causes an increase in the autonomy and flexibility of the client's behavior. "The ends justify the means." Foreman (1990) believes that "paradox is an ethical technique with resistive clients" and advises that the paradoxical approach be used only after other approaches have been unsuccessful.

* * *

Manipulation for therapeutic and altruistic motives has been sanctioned by leading Jewish religious leaders, although it was condemned when used for selfish interests because the values of integrity and honesty are paramount.

(An example of the latter is found in Tractate Yevamot (63a): The wife of Rav (one of the outstanding scholars in the Talmudic era) was in the habit of irritating him. When he requested from his wife to cook for him lentils, he received chick-peas and when he requested chick-peas, he would receive lentils. When his son Chiyah grew up, he reversed his father's requests to his mother. Rav said to his son: 'Your mother has improved'. His son said: 'I reversed the requests to her'. His father said to him. 'This is what people say, that your son teaches you wisdom. Even so, don't do this, because it is written in Jeremiah, 'Their tongues will teach deceitful things.'"

Rashi (11th century biblical commentator) in his commentary on *Ethics of the Fathers* (1:2) records the strategic-manipulative interventions of Aaron the High Priest, who pursued peace and infused love between disputants and between quarrelling spouses, and who antedated Haley and Erickson, two of the most prominent strategic therapists, by 3300 years.

"One man became angry with his wife and chased her out of the house and swore that he would permit her to return only if she spat in the face of the High Priest. When Aaron became aware of this, he summoned the woman and told her that he had an eye infection which could only be cured if she spat at it. After considerable pleading, the woman acceded to Aaron's request. Afterwards, Aaron summoned the husband and related to him what his wife had done. As a result of this, the couple reconciled."

"When two men quarreled, Aaron would go to one of the disputants and inform him that he had just returned from the disputant's friend and found him terribly upset and regretful of the pain that he had caused his fellow. Aaron would not leave the disputant until all jealousy and hatred had been removed from his heart. Afterwards, he would go to the other injured party and repeat the same thing to him. When the men met, they would fall on each other's shoulders and tearfully reconcile.

* * *

The most well known and psychologically sophisticated manipulative intervention by a Jewish religious leader recorded in the Scriptures, is described in Kings-1 (3, 15-28), regarding King Solomon's judgment in the dispute between two women contesting the maternity of the live child.

Several examples are recorded in the Talmud of manipulative behavior by prominent religious figures whose intentions were to help fellow Jews. It is related in Tractate Nedarim (50a) that the Prophet Elijah appeared at Rabbi Akiva's dwelling (a barn where he and his wife slept on straw) as a pauper and requested some straw for his wife who had recently given birth to lie down on. Rabbi Nissim explains that Elijah did this in order to console the couple and show them there were people poorer than themselves.

In Tractate Yevamot (11b) it is recorded that the Sages advised a woman to "playact" (to cry, tear her clothing, and dishevel her hair) when she appeared before Rabbi Judah in order to convince him that her husband had died, so that he would permit her to remarry.

In Tractate Arachin (23a), it is related that Moses the son of Etsri was the guarantor for the marriage contract of his daughter-in-law. His son, Rabbi Huna, was a scholar with little financial resources. Abaye said: "Is there no one to advise Rabbi Huna to divorce his wife and since he is without means, his wife will collect the money from his father and afterwards Rabbi Huna will remarry her. This way he will be able to support her and himself." The Talmud explains that this kind of conspiracy is permissible when it is done for the benefit of a son who is a scholar.

* * *

Rabbi Ezkiel Landau, (18th century prominent rabbinic scholar and author) did not believe in amulets or in other supernatural remedies. Once he was consulted regarding an amulet. A distinguished woman was seized by a spirit of insanity. She felt that her condition was critical, and that she could be remedied only with an amulet prepared by Rabbi Ezkiel. Rabbi Ezkiel took a blank piece of parchment, wrapped it in a small pouch, sealed it with his personal signet, and said: "This amulet should be worn around the neck of the woman for thirty days. After thirty days, open the amulet. If the writing disappeared and the parchment is blank, it is a sign that the woman is remedied. And so they did. After thirty days they opened the amulet and found the parchment blank with no sign of any script. The woman entirely recuperated from her illness.

* * *

Another example of another psychologically sophisticated intervention by a prominent rabbinic figure of the 19th century, is recorded by Karlinsky. (1984) The incident took place in Warsaw in 1877. Rabbi Joseph Dov Soloveitchik, an outstanding Talmud scholar, religious personality, and leader was overcome by a deep depression upon the incarceration of his highly revered and beloved mentor, Rabbi Joshua Leib Diskin, on false charges by the anti-Semitic authorities. On the Sabbath Rabbi Soloveitchik ate only the minimal amount of food necessary to fulfill the requirements of Jewish law. He isolated himself in his room and refused to receive any visitors, not even his closest students and colleagues. He discontinued going to the synagogue and teaching. A specialist who was called in to treat him recommended total rest, but added that if by chance the rabbi's spirit could be suddenly stimulated, healing would take place in a matter of minutes.

Attempts by his family, friends, students, and colleagues to pull him out of his depression failed. Even the efforts of the renowned scholar and hasidic leader, the Master of Gur, failed to lift his colleague's depression through encouragement, support, and intellectual stimulation. One day, upon hearing about Rabbi Soloveitchik's deteriorating mental and physical condition, Rabbi Meir Simha Ha'Kohen, a brilliant scholar and student of Rabbi Soloveitchik, hurried to visit his teacher. Rabbi Meir attempted unsuccessfully to engage his rabbi in a talmudic discussion, as the latter was totally engulfed by worry for his beloved colleague. At one point, Rabbi Meir quoted some of the Torah novella that he had heard from Rabbi Diskin when he had visited him in jail some months previously. As Rabbi Meir discerned some reaction from his teacher, he began to challenge and criticize Rabbi Diskin's new insights and interpretations on certain talmudic topics and vigorously disputed the conclusions. Upon hearing criticism of his beloved teacher, Rabbi Soloveitchik began to defend him by quoting texts and rabbinical authorities and explaining and analyzing his teacher's Torah. Instead of remitting, Rabbi Meir continued to challenge Rabbi Diskin's Torah, which prompted Rabbi Soloveitchik to raise his voice and marshal all his brilliance, analytic skills, and energy to refute his student's arguments and prove that his mentor was correct. Rabbi Meir soon began to raise other talmudic topics to which Rabbi Soloveitchik also responded in an increasingly intense manner.

After concluding their talmudic deliberations, Rabbi Soloveitchik accompanied his visitor to the synagogue, where he had not gone for a long time. Shortly afterward, Rabbi Soloveitchik resumed his teaching and regular activities as the spiritual leader of his community.

Another example of a creative manipulative intervention on the part of a respected rabbinic figure is an incident related about Rabbi Mordechai Lebton, the Chief Rabbi and head of the rabbinical court in Syria in the nineteenth century. One day a distraught couple appeared before the rabbi for a divorce. Though the couple had been happily married for many years, during the last year the husband had become depressed, angry, and impatient with his wife because she was barren and therefore decided to divorce her. The rabbi unsuccessfully attempted to persuade the husband to reconsider his decision since his wife was a fine meritorious person.

The rabbi, a highly intelligent and perceptive person who was able to penetrate the inner recesses of people and discern their dynamics and weaknesses, decided on a plan of action to cause the husband to revive his affection and appreciation of his wife. He instructed the couple to return the following day for the purpose of arranging the divorce procedures.

The next day, as the rabbi was preparing to divorce the couple, his student (upon pre-arranged instructions) barged in and whispered into the rabbi's ear. The rabbi unexpectedly began scolding and yelling at his student to the astonishment of the estranged couple. When queried about his unusual behavior, the rabbi explained that his student had crossed the line of propriety. "My student had the audacity to ask me to hasten the divorce proceedings so that he could propose marriage to this wonderful woman."

Upon hearing this, the shocked husband informed the rabbi that he decided to return to his wife and asked the rabbi for his blessing. The following year, a son was born to the happy couple.

The "Hafetz Haim" (the most prominent rabbinical authority of the 20th century) was consulted about how to help a young scholar, who had a fine personality, came from a good family, but was of short stature, which made it difficult to find him a suitable wife. The rabbi advised that he should wear elevated shoes at the first meeting in order to give him a taller appearance but not afterwards. The explanation given was that the potential mate should not be repelled and discouraged on first sight and that after getting to know him, his physical stature would not be a significant decisive factor.

It appears that the rabbinic attitude regarding the ends justifying the means is quite flexible, as they sanction and use manipulation when noble goals are involved such as the enhancement of people's emotional and social well-being.

References

Chazan, R. (2000) Book Review: "Cotherapy with individuals, families and groups". Israel Journal of Psychiatry, 37, 1.

Doherty, W. J. & Boss, P. G. (1991) Values and ethics in family therapy. In A. S. Gurman & D. P. Kniskern (Eds.) Handbook of family therapy (vol. 2), New York: Brunner/Mazel.

Foreman, D. M. (1990) The ethical use of paradoxical interventions in psychotherapy. Journal of Medical Ethics, 16, 200-205.

Haley, J. (1976) Problem-solving therapy. San-Francisco, Jossey-Bass.

Hoffman, S., Gafni, S. and Laub, B. (1994) Cotherapy with individuals, families and groups, Northvale, New Jersey, Jason Aronson, Inc.

Karlinsky, C. (1984) The first of the Brisk dynasty. Jerusalem: Jerusalem Institute. (In Hebrew).

4

"Kosher" Talebearing:
A Modest Proposal

Gossip: A Universal Problem

The two dominant and strongest drives, needs, and urges that propel a human being are: 1. Survival (eating, drinking); and 2. Sex. The attitude of Judaism toward human impulses and needs is a balanced one. Our impulses and needs should not be eradicated or denied but acknowledged, channeled, sublimated, and expressed in a controlled and responsible manner.

A man should conquer his passions, and is warned not to say, "By nature, I do not lust after prohibited things—I am repulsed by meat mixed with milk, I am repulsed by shatnez, I am repulsed by forbidden sexual unions."Say instead, "They are attractive, but what can I do? My Father in Heaven has forbidden them!" (Torat Kohanim, Kedoshin, 9)

The Talmud records that the wife of Rabbi Nahman asked her husband, "For everything prohibited by the Torah there is something similar to it that is permitted. Blood is prohibited while the liver of the animal is permitted; fat from an animal is prohibited while fat from a kosher beast is permitted; another man's wife is prohibited while a divorced woman in the lifetime of her former husband is permitted; a Gentile woman is prohibited but a captive woman during war is permitted.... Consumption of meat and milk together, wherefore?" Talmud Hullin 109b.

One could ask, "Talebearing, wherefore?"

The Torah clearly forbids talebearing (gossip, slander, squealing, lashon ha'ra):

> Thou shall not go about as a talebearer among the people. (Leviticus 19:16).

According to the Ḥafets Ḥayyim, talebearing includes both saying something bad about a person (lashon ha'ra) and telling a person that another person did something bad to him or spoke badly about him (reḥilut). The above acts are prohibited even if what was said is true.[1]

One who speaks or hears lashon ha'ra, according to the Ḥafets Ḥayyim, may transgress thirty-one commandments—fourteen positive and seventeen negative commandments.[2] Our sages consider lashon ha'ra a sin equivalent to idolatry, murder, and prohibited sexual relations, as it causes conflict, division, animosity, and unwarranted hate among people.[3]

Talebearing is so powerful an urge and drive that few people are capable of withstanding its strong pull. Even Miriam the prophetess succumbed to it and was severely punished for gossiping about her illustrious brother Moses.[4]

The Talmud says: The Holy One said to the tongue, "All the limbs of man are vertical, and you are horizontal. All the limbs of man are external, and you are internal. Not only that, but I surrounded you with two walls, one of bone and one of flesh. What more can be given to you and what more can be added to you, deceitful tongue [to stop you from sinning]?" Talmud Arakhin 15b.

"Kosher" Talebearing

In the spirit of Rabbi Naḥman's wife, a possible solution to the dilemma of talebearing may be offered in which something similar to the forbidden act is permitted. A colleague of mine related to me a

---

1 Ḥafets Ḥayyim, Lavin 1.
2 Ibid., Lavin 1-17, Asiyin 1-14.
3 *Talmud* Arakhin 15b.
4 Numbers 12.

charming story of a group of strictly religious women in Hungary at the beginning of the twentieth century. Perturbed by their strong urge to gossip, the righteous women found a unique solution to their dilemma. Every week they met over a cup of coffee to discuss and analyze the main characters of a literary work that they had read. In dissecting and analyzing the fictitious characters, they found an outlet to express, project, give vent to their pent-up feelings, frustrations, fantasies, and anger, while discharging their strong urge to speak and hear lashon ha'ra in a socially and halakhically acceptable manner, without causing distress and harm to anyone.

There are several defense mechanisms in operation here. Defense mechanisms are automatic psychological processes that protect the individual from anxiety and from awareness of internal or external stressors or dangers by mediating the person's reactions to the latter. Some are maladaptive and others are adaptive, depending on their severity, inflexibility, and the context in which they occur. Several ways that an individual may deal with emotional conflict or internal or external stressors are by: 1. *Displacement.* A feeling about or a response to one object is transferred to a substitute (usually less threatening) object. 2. *Projection.* One's own unacceptable feelings, impulses, or thoughts are falsely attributed to another. 3. *Sublimation.* Potentially maladaptive feelings or angry, aggressive impulses are channeled into socially acceptable behavior (such as being a boxer, a butcher, or a surgeon).[5]

Modest Proposal

Various weekly or monthly (depending on the intensity of the gossip urge) "literary" discussion groups be organized. Each group should be homogeneous according to background, intelligence, age, gender,

---

5 See Diagnostic and Statistical Manual of Mental Disorders, 4th ed., (American Psychiatric Association, 1994), 751-757.

and so forth to enable men and women to give expression to their need to gossip in an indirect and halakhically acceptable manner. The choice of literary focus would depend on the levels and interests of the group participants. One group may choose to focus on the ancient classics, another on appropriate contemporary works, others on light novels or short stories, while others may choose to bring in their own literary efforts. These meetings will not only enable the participants to gossip with a clear conscience but also facilitate socialization, encourage reading good literature, increase knowledge, and provide a healthy forum for ventilation and catharsis.

Addendum

Below are the findings of a study (Glinert, L., Loewenthal, K. M. and Goldblat, V., 2004) that reports the views and experiences of Strictly-Orthodox Jewish women with respect to the meta-pragmatic ethos of Shmiras HaLoshon (monitoring one's talk, literally 'guarding the tongue'). Eight extended interviews were conducted with Strictly-Orthodox women and teenagers in London, and salient themes were identified, namely:

A. Loshon Hora ('evil talk') is the prime exemplar of bad talk.
B. Loshon Hora is the hardest (one of the hardest) things to avoid, because it is so easy to do.
C. The perceived consequences of Loshon Hora are very serious
D. Great caution/various strategies are employed in order to not speak Loshon Hora
E. Perceived gender differences exist in proneness to speak Loshon Hora.
F. One is reponsible for monitoring others.
G. Young children can be(come) aware of the issues.

Subjects appeared to take this aspect of religious observance very seriously, and were taking active steps to promote observance. Social desirability bias may be an inappropriate concept for explaining our participants' behaviour. It is also suggested that the perceived importance of Shmiras HaLoshon may be important in helping to maintain community cohesion and preventing conflicts, by improving respect for privacy and reputation in a community where gossip is attractive but divisive.

References

Glinert, L., Loewenthal, K. M. and Goldblat, V. (2004) Guarding the tongue: A thematic analysis of gossip control strategies among orthodox Jewish women in London, Journal of Multilingual and Multicultural Development, 5, 24, 3.

5

"Helpmate Unto Him":
Dialectical Cotherapy

Introduction

Jewish biblical commentators throughout the centuries have given us keen insights into the psychological makeup of marriage. This may be seen by studying commentary on the second half of Genesis 2:20, "But for Adam there was not found a helpmate for him" For "helpmate" the Hebrew text uses the two words, "ezer k' negdo". The root of "neged" means "opposite" or "against."

The Netsiv (Rabbi Naftali Tsvi Yehuda Berlin, 1817-1893) comments, "Adam understood after he realized his limitations that he needed a helpmate with forces, but oppositional forces that would be a help to him (ezer k'negdo), a help if she is against him-to moderate his traits, and in this manner together they will achieve completeness."

On this same verse Rabbi Samson Raphael Hirsch (1808-1888) comments, "Because the wife is to be the helpmate of her husband, she must be opposite him; because she is to complement him, she must have different characteristics than his."

Nahmanides (Rabbi Moshe ben Nahman, 1194-1270) interprets ezer k'negdo as "opposite, distinct from."

The "Ktav Sofer" (Abraham Sofer, 1815-1871), in his commentary on the book of Exodus, makes an interesting observation regarding the two leaders ("parents") of the Jewish people, Moses and Aaron.

"The redemption required two leaders, each with a different personality. In order to speak to the hearts of the children of Israel that they will believe in the redemption, required a messenger with a good temperament who would comfort the people, sweeten their difficulties, strengthen their spirit and hope for redemption. For this, Aaron stood out, since he would be listened to because he was accepted by the people, because he loved and pursued peace. In contrast, in external affairs with Pharaoh, a messenger with strong willpower and endurance that fulfills his task fearlessly, is required. For this, Moses stood out, for he spoke to Pharaoh impudently: "In order that thou know that the earth is the Lord's" (Exodus, 9, 29); "Thou must also give into our hand sacrifices and burnt-offerings" (Exodus, 10, 25); I will see thy face again no more" (Exodus, 10, 29).

The above insights are further analyzed and explicated by the popular psychology author and psychotherapist, Sheldon Kopp. (1972) Reflecting the prevalent views of social scientists today, Kopp says that to some extent people marry to make up for their own deficiencies. We seek the missing half of ourselves, our missing rib. Each of us is in some measure incomplete, with some aspects of our humanity overdeveloped and other aspects neglected. An aggressive person seeks a gentle person; a spontaneous spirit seeks a stable anchor.

If people married spouses just like themselves, disasters might well ensue. Two timid souls would justify each other's cautiousness until neither ventured anything new. An adventuresome pair might escalate each other's recklessness into a spiral of catastrophes.

The differences between spouses are both the strength of a good marriage and the hazards of a bad one. Ironically, we marry the other because he (she) is different from us, and then we complain that he (she) is not like us. We complain bitterly about having to live with a mate who is acting exactly in the way that he (she) found most attractive during courtship!

Dialectical Cotherapy

The above insights and views gave birth to the development of a psychotherapeutic approach known as "dialectical cotherapy." This approach exploits the different and contrasting traits and functions of cotherapists in their simultaneous treatment of individuals, couples, and families. (Hoffman, et.al., 1994).

In classical philosophy, "dialectic is controversy: the exchange of arguments and counter-arguments respectively advocating propositions (theses) and counter-propositions (antitheses). The outcome of the exercise might not simply be the refutation of one of the relevant points of view, but a synthesis or combination of the opposing assertions, or at least a qualitative transformation in the direction of the dialogue". (Ayer and O'Grady, 1992)

According to psychotherapist Marcia Linehan, "dialectics" refers to the process of change that occurs through the simultaneous considerations of opposing viewpoints. (Linehan, 1991).

Haim Omer (1991) views dialectical interventions as "treatment strategies that embody two antithetical moves in such a way that as the pendulum swings from one side to another, change forces are mobilized and resistances neutralized. These interventions consist of two coordinated contrary movements that may be thought of as a thesis and an antithesis. Although sometimes the intervention aims at giving maximum power to one of the polar movements, at other times, it aims at an emerging synthesis."

Winnicott (1971) coined the term "transitional phenomena", which refers to an in-between space which takes place in the process of the development of the self, and indicates the achievement of the ability of subjective experience. This potential space comes into existence in a dialectical process which combines inner reality and outer reality in a way that reflects neither of them but a new entity which is a synergic outcome of the two. It happens in the child's life by moving from a dyadic to a triadic relationship acquiring "the third position", which is an important milestone in self-development. Here we see again the power of the dialectical process that creates a new qualitative entity out of two opposing vectors.

Regarding the above treatment approach, Laub (2001) has suggested a model that deals with the application of the universal polarity to the therapeutic situation. "Polarity is a central concept in Eastern and Western cultures. The concept of polarity is one of the main elements in the Kabbalah and is described as the male element (right side) and the female element (left side)."

The male-female polarity plays an important role in the process of socialization. Children, unwittingly, are influenced by the contrasting attitudes and behaviors of their parents toward them and the significant people in their environment. Father and mother represent two models for relationship; the mother expresses unconditional love and acceptance and provides the child with emotional encouragement and support while the father expresses expectation, responsibility, limitations and discipline. The former fulfills the nurturing role, the latter, the instrumental role. The former provides for the child's emotional needs so that he/she can cope with life's challenges and demands, the latter, the tools. Both contrasting and complementary influences are vital in order to ensure that the child grows up to be a healthy and contented person.

In the dialectical cotherapy approach, the therapists actively interact with each other and with their clients. They share their views, feelings and perceptions in front of the clients, model selective behavior, role-play, intentionally take opposing sides on issues, and sometimes participate in paradoxical interventions. One therapist is supportive, nurturing and empathic, while the other is confronting and challenging. The former relates to the affective needs, wishes and fantasies of the client, emphasizes her strengths, positive attributes and desire and capability to change and grow, while the latter relates more to the negative aspects, obstacles and fears and is skeptical about her motivation and capacity for meaningful change. He is more instrumental, goal and reality oriented and challenges the client to prove him wrong. This approach promotes, in a quick and effective manner, the uncovering of underlying conflicts and ambivalence and makes them more readily available for therapeutic work and resolution. As Whitaker has put it: "One therapist performs the surgery and the other the anesthesia". (1977)

* * *

Below is presented a brief description of the dialectical cotherapy approach with a four year old selective mutistic girl. Selective mutism, formerly called elective mutism, is defined as a disorder of childhood characterized by an inability to speak in certain settings (e.g. at school, in public places) despite speaking in other settings (e.g. at home with family). Selectively mute children can be divided into two groups: 1) those who use refusal to speak in a coercive fashion in order to manipulate people and the immediate environment, and 2) those for whom speaking is sufficiently anxiety producing so the child chooses to remain mute (Friedman and Kagan, 1973).

Rosenberg and Lindblad (1978) list the following observations regarding choice of symptom and underlying dynamics of selectively mute children: 1) the child is extremely determined to hold onto his symptom and has an overwhelming need to control; 2) the symptom becomes an extremely effective passive-aggressive maneuver by the child and arouses extreme feelings of anger, frustration, and disappointment in the parents; 3) the home atmosphere is not conducive to expression of feelings. Although the age of onset is usually before five, the disturbance may come to clinical attention only with entry to school. Therefore, the symptom may already be a routine of the child and more or less accepted by his surroundings.

The literature on the treatment of selective mutism tends to focus on the anxiety or family dynamic component of the symptom and little attention is directed to the controlling, manipulating, negativistic, passive-aggressive component. Below is presented a case study of a four year old selectively mute child who was treated successfully by cotherapists using a dialectical cotherapy approach.

Case Study

Lily, a four-and-a-half year old kindergarten girl, was referred to the clinic because of her refusal to speak to adults, with the exception of her parents and four grandparents. In school she spoke only with the children and used her closest friend as an intermediary when communicating with the teacher.

Lily's family consists of parents, age 30, and a seven year-old brother named Eli. At approximately age two, Lily was hospitalized for two weeks because of a serious case of ataxia. The parents described the hospitalization as traumatic both for them and for the child, even though the child recovered quickly. The parents reported that from that time on, Lily refused to talk and avoided contact with adults although even before that time she had tended to cry when grownups outside the immediate family approached her. The referring psychologist, who had treated the family for a year using a "structural family therapy approach and educational guidance," described the child as possessing at least average intelligence.

Before the initial meeting with the family, the authors decided to avoid getting into a power struggle with the child (and continue to do "more of the same") and to relate to her in a totally different manner than, we presumed, she anticipated. In the first session, after the formal introductions, the therapists informed the parents that they do not speak to young children and that if they wished to tell Lily something (or she them), the therapists would use the parents as intermediaries.

Throughout the first and subsequent meetings, Lily attached herself to her mother and avoided contact with the therapists. In the third session, the therapists expressed their belief to the family and to the two sets of grandparents, who had been invited to that meeting, that Lily had a good reason for refusing to speak to adults although they themselves were not certain of the reason. Several hypotheses were offered: her speech was infantile and, therefore, she was afraid that adults outside the immediate family constellation would laugh at her; or that she felt that the family wanted an infant in the house; or that it could be her way of uniting the entire family by having them preoccupied with her "disability;" or it could be her way of notifying the family that she did not wish to grow up and leave the warmth and security of the home. In this meeting the therapists also emphasized the importance of ceasing to pressure her to speak to adults. (The grandfather, for example, promised her an expensive talking doll if she spoke to adults). Following this meeting, the therapists met with the kindergarten teacher and received her promise to cooperate in not pressuring the child to speak to her.

In subsequent sessions with the nuclear family, there developed a contrived split between the two therapists. The "bad" male therapist took the stance that Lily was an infant and, therefore, was not able to speak to adults, and that it was important to the family that she remain this way since the parents did not plan to have any more children. The "good" female therapist, in contrast, expressed the belief that Lily was capable of mature behavior and encouraged the family to start relating to her in accordance with her age. The "good" therapist lavishly praised the child and parents when they reported that their daughter began eating by herself, helped with the dishes, and so on. The male therapist continued to express doubt about the child's achievements and pointed to her clinging and childlike behavior in the room as proof that she was an infant.

In the following session Lily refused to enter the office, and in contrast with previous times, the therapists permitted the behavior.

During the middle of the session the female therapist left the room to answer the telephone and exploited the situation to whisper several words to the child and to give her a hug. When the female therapist returned, the male therapist sent Eli out with a message to his sister that he did not believe the parents' report that she put together a 50-piece puzzle by herself, because little children are not able to do such a difficult task. The brother returned with his sister's response, "The psychologist is an idiot." This was the first obvious breach in the child's detachment facade and armor.

At the next meeting, Lily presented to the therapists via the parents a picture of a fruit tree that she had drawn. Though the therapists both admired the drawing, the male therapist expressed doubt that she had drawn it since she was so immature, while the female therapist and family members insisted that she did draw it and that she was capable of mature and age-appropriate behavior. The parents also pointed out that the kindergarten teacher was also impressed by the child's artistic ability.

An argument ensued between the therapists regarding the child's ability to speak maturely. The male therapist insisted that she was only able to babble and make sounds like aah, baa, vaa, daa, and so on, while the female therapist insisted that she was capable of mature speech. They decided to bet 100 shekels on who was right, and told the family that they would return in a few minutes and listen to the tape that they had inserted in the tape recorder to determine who won the bet. After hearing the child's voice on the tape, the male therapist grudgingly gave a 100 shekel bill to his cotherapist, even though he protested that Lily's speech was not very loud or clear and did not give evidence that she was able to speak in full sentences. At this point, the female therapist asked the father to bring to the next session a tape recording of Lily speaking, to which he acceded.

After hearing the child's voice on the tape at the following session, the male therapist admitted that he had erred, but still insisted that she was immature in that she was not able to speak in the presence of adults not of the immediate family. He then challenged Eli to bet him candies on whether Lily would be able to speak in the presence of the female therapist after he absented himself from the room. The female therapist expressed confidence that Lily would be able to accomplish the task and Eli agreed to the bet. Upon hearing Lily's voice on the tape recorder after returning to the office, the male therapist reluctantly placed candy in the hands of the smiling children. The "defeated" therapist, however, persisted and challenged Eli again to bet him on whether his sister would be able to speak directly even one word to the female therapist in his absence. He again accepted the challenge, but this time lost the bet as Lily was only able to open her mouth, but could not emit any words. The male therapist gloated over his victory and collected his prize from the dejected children.

At the end of the session, the male therapist proclaimed that his primary interest was to acquire as much candy as possible and was unconcerned whether the girl spoke or not, and in a provocative manner challenged Eli to a further bet. The therapist took out a bag of candy and said that if Lily would speak one word to the kindergarten teacher by the time they returned to the next meeting the candy would be theirs. A letter from the teacher attesting to this was required. If not, they would have to give him a bag of candy. Again the female therapist expressed confidence in the child's ability to succeed in this assigned task and after agreeing to the bet, Eli was given the bag of candy for safekeeping.

Several days later, the father appeared unexpectedly with a large grin on his face, shook the male therapist's hand, kissed the female therapist and with great emotion, revealed that Lily not only spoke to the kindergarten teacher but also to other adults. We smiled approvingly and told him the children could eat the candy to celebrate their victory. We cautioned him however, to relate to this new phenomenon in a natural manner.

In the final session, (18th), the parents presented the therapists with chocolate and a small celebration was held, which was the culmination of a long chain of festivities sponsored by the kindergarten teacher and various family members. The celebrations reminded us of a "Bat Mitzvah" ceremony (when a Jewish girl reaches the age of adulthood and responsibility), as if Lily had received the family's permission and blessing to grow and mature. (In relation to this, the grandmother of the child exclaimed to the female therapist whom she met several days later, "It's coming to me a 'mazal tov'" (congratulations).

In response to the female therapist's question, the child explained that the reason she did not speak to adults in the past was that she had a sore throat and last week it stopped hurting. The therapists noted that the bag of candy that she won was still unopened as if the child was going to hold on to her "trophy". At the end of the session, the male therapist apologized profusely to the child for thinking that she was an infant and asked for her forgiveness. Lily timidly shook the therapist's extended hand, and thus accepted him to the list of adults with whom she conversed.

In a follow-up meeting two months later, the parents reported that Lily had stopped using a pacifier, extended the list of adults with whom she speaks, expanded her circle of friends in kindergarten, and was displaying more independent and age appropriate behavior.

Discussion

In the case of Lily, two components of the selective mutism symptom were present, anxiety and control. While the former may have been central at the beginning, it appears that the latter component became more prominent after a while as a result of secondary gains obtained from the environment.

In view of the aforementioned, we elected at the beginning of the treatment process to use a paradoxical approach which included re-defining the symptom and refraining from attempting to remove it.

As a result of these interventions, the decreased attention given to the symptom and increased provocations on the part of the male therapist, Lily was "unbalanced" and the effect and strength of her symptom was diminished significantly. In order to re-establish and regain power and control, the child had to prove to the male therapist that he erred. Had she refused to take part in the "gambling game," it would have been an admission that he was right and that she was truly a helpless infant who was incapable of speaking to adults. The "triumph" over the male therapist regained for her the control and power but in a more constructive and appropriate way.

The stance taken by the "good" therapist was directed primarily at decreasing the anxiety component of the symptom through actions aimed at strengthening self-confidence and self-esteem, while the position of the "bad" therapist was primarily directed toward the control/defiance component of the symptom through the use of defiance based paradoxical interventions. The male therapist's provocative behavior also angered the child and thereby forced her to become involved in the therapy sessions. The positive attitude of the female therapist enabled Lily to continue attending the sessions and to begin experimenting with age appropriate behavior. The provocations of the male therapist indirectly encouraged the child to "join" the "good" therapist in order to defeat the "bad" therapist. At this point, behavioral techniques such as reinforcement, counter-conditioning, and successive approximations were effective in decreasing the child's anxiety in regard to speaking to adults.

The father, who was an electrician by trade, explained the therapeutic process in professional terminology. While there was a positive connection between Lily and the female therapist, there was a short circuit between her and the male therapist. In reference to this, the father related that Lily was extremely upset and furious at the male therapist's remark that he was only interested in acquiring candy and not in whether she spoke or not. This provocation caused her to speak to the kindergarten teacher and to other adults in order to prevent him from winning more candy and to prove him wrong. The father concluded that there was a need for a plus and minus in the therapeutic situation in order to induce an electrical current (change of a static situation). Two pluses ("good" therapists) or two minuses ("bad" therapists) would not have produced, in his view, the same results.

References

Ayer, A. J., and O'Grady, J. (1992). A dictionary of philosophical quotations. Oxford, UK: Blackwell Publishers, p. 484.

Friedman, R. & Kagan, N. (1973) Characteristics and management of elective mutism in children. Psychology in the Schools ,10, 249-252.

Hoffman, S., Gafni, S. and Laub, B. (1994) Cotherapy with Individuals, Families and Groups. New Jersey, Jason Aronson, Inc.

Laub, B. (2001) Who is in the therapy room? The dialectical connection between therapist-client. Problem-healing force. Nefesh, 8, 43-52. (Hebrew).

Linehan, M. M. (1991) Cognitive-behavioral Treatment for Borderline Personality Disorder. New York, Guilford Press.

Omer, H. (1991) Dialectical Interventions and The Structure Of Strategy. Psychotherapy, 28, (4), 563-571.

Rosenberg, B. J. & Lindblad, M. B. (1978) Behavior therapy in a family context: Treating elective mutism. Family Process, 17, 77-82.

Whitaker, C. A. (1997) Process techniques of family therapy. Interaction.1, 4-19.

Winnicott, D. W. (1971) Playing and Reality. New York: Basic Books.

6

Rabbis and Psychologists:
"And They Both Walked Together"?

The attitude of orthodox rabbis toward mental health practitioners varies from outright hostility and distrust to respect and cooperation. Those identified with the ultra-orthodox camp generally view psychotherapists as a threat to religion and religious values, while modern orthodox rabbis generally relate to them as colleagues in ministering to the emotional and psychological needs of people in distress. The former group, generally, is highly vocal in its condemnation and criticism, while the latter group, generally, is rather subdued and guarded in its support of them.

Ultra-orthodox pronouncements vary from temperate, cautious criticism and advice, to ridicule and belittlement, to venomous accusations and outright prohibitions against seeking psychotherapists' counsel.

"It is forbidden to go to a psychologist or psychiatrist who is a heretic or atheist... one must seek out a psychologist or psychiatrist who keeps the Torah. If this is not possible, then one can even go to a heretic or atheist, but it must be stipulated and he must promise not to discuss matters of belief and the Torah with the patient." (*Igrot Moshe, Yoreh De'ah*, 2:57).

"Even the best therapists have nothing to offer those whose sins have brought them to depression or sadness, for the help they need is from those knowledgeable in Torah, who are the real healers of souls... Psychologists and psychiatrists steal a lot of money from the patient and let him imagine that he will be healed." (*Tshuvot VeHanhagot*, 1:465, Rabbi Moses Sternbuch).

The haredi newspaper "*Yated Ne'eman*" reported on a halachic ruling by Rabbi Shmuel Auerbach, head of the *Ma'alot haTorah* Yeshiva in Jerusalem, that prohibited psychological counseling because "psychological treatment is the advice of the devil and the evil impulse and a terrible obstacle."

In the Jewish Tribune, an orthodox newspaper in England, Rabbi Shmuel Wosner, a recognized decisor from Bnei Brak, was quoted as stating, "their (psychologists) advice is the counsel of the wicked and it usually results in evil."

In his "Mishneh Halachot" (part 4, p. 127), Rabbi Menashe Hakatan (Klein) cites an article by Rabbi Moshe Deutch, head of the Katamon Religious court in London, entitled, "Turn not to soothsayers in the guise of psychologists", where the author makes several points: 1. Rabbi S. Z. Auerbach was of the opinion that "going to them (psychologists) results in much corruption"; 2. The Hazon Ish explicitly stated that one should not go to psychologists because they corrupt more than they repair; 3. The author of "Kehilat Yaacov" was of the same opinion.

In response to a question posed to him at a lecture he delivered at the Annual "Nefesh Israel" Conference (2004), Rabbi Yehoshua Neuwirth responded, "It is prohibited to refer patients to psychiatrists. Psychiatrists stupefy the soul."

At a conference held at Bar-Ilan University (March, 2005), entitled, "Professional Collaboration between Rabbis and Psychologists", in which rabbis and mental health practitioners participated, three prominent national religious rabbis presented their views on the above subject.

Rabbi Yisroel Meir Lau, former chief rabbi of Israel and presently chief rabbi of Tel-Aviv, pointed out that the relationship between rabbis and psychologists is in principle similar to that between halacha and medicine but stressed the difference between the objective physician and the subjective psychologist. "The psychologist", he said, "does not operate in a bubble, and something of his faith, his world view and values are also imprinted on his treatment methods."

Rabbi Shlomo Aviner, head of the Ateret Cohanim Yeshiva in Jerusalem, and rabbi of the settlement Bet El, opined that "halacha and psychology are two different worlds that can go together despite the fact that they speak two different languages", continuing the same line. "The psychologist deals with that that exists, whereas the rabbi deals with that that should exist."

Rabbi Yaacov Ariel, chief rabbi of Ramat Gan, put an even finer point on the matter. "The problem is that the psychologist suggests to the patient that he comes to terms with reality, whereas the rabbi suggests that he perfect the reality. If the psychologists continue to propose to the patients to come to terms with reality, the rabbis will continue to hesitate about referring people to them."

Isolated reactions in support of psychological treatment argue that, "Amateur dabbling in this area (psychotherapy) causes negative outcomes and may, God forbid, lead to suicide," and, "before telling people with phobias, depression and obsessive-compulsive disorders to consult their rabbis and not their psychologists, success rates for rabbis for particular conditions ought to be objectively assessed and published."(1)

Several actual examples of negative outcomes as a result of "amateur dabbling" by rabbis are presented below.

1. A woman who was hospitalized several times in a psychiatric hospital with a diagnosis of schizophrenia was told by a well-known kabbalist with whom she had consulted, that the voices she hears were that of an angel who was punishing her for her transgressions and that she should repent. This declaration was in sharp contrast to her therapist's attempts to convince the patient that the voices she hears were imaginary and that this was her way of attempting to deal with her unacceptable thoughts and feelings. While the former was reinforcing the patient's pathology and guilt feelings, the latter was attempting to help the patient

strengthen her ability to test reality and diminish her intense guilt feelings and suicidal ideations.

2. A father consulted his rabbi regarding his daughter who was suffering from depression and was not functioning for over a year. The rabbi cautioned the father against consulting a psychiatrist and advised him to change the mezzuzot in his house. When his daughter's condition didn't improve after he acquired new mezzuzot, the father sought professional help.

3. A student sought his rabbi's advice regarding his uncertainty about marrying his fiancée after he noticed that she was extremely preoccupied with cleanliness (she avoided touching objects that fell on the floor, spent considerable time washing, etc.). The rabbi assured his student that his fiancée would stop this "foolishness" after her marriage. A month after the wedding, the student's wife was hospitalized with a diagnosis of severe obsessive-compulsive disorder and a year later, the couple separated.

Clergymen and clinicians have something of value to offer to each other to enhance the quality of their assistance to the people they serve. Therefore it is extremely important that both professions recognize the limits of their own professional competence and consider the benefits of working and consulting with each other.

Interdisciplinary collaboration between clergymen and mental health practitioners — especially psychotherapists — in treating emotionally disturbed patients is a rare phenomenon. One explanation for this is the relative ignorance of and unfamiliarity with each other's field and area of concern. This tends to produce anxiety, doubt, suspicion, and mutual distrust.

Bi-directional programs of education and collaboration should be developed and offered to clergymen and clinicians. (2) By providing clergy with some basic knowledge and exposure to psychopathology and psychiatric and psychological treatment, they will develop a greater appreciation for the complexity of the human mind and psychotherapy, and will be in a better position to make more appropriate referrals and provide supportive counseling to their emotionally disordered and distressed parishioners. Likewise, a basic knowledge of religious laws, customs, values and rituals will enable psychotherapists to better appreciate the benefits of religious belief and conduct to mental health and make more effective and appropriate diagnoses, referrals and interventions in their clinical work.

In regards to the latter point, the potential deleterious effect of a significant lacuna in the knowledge of religious laws and rituals of the clinician was demonstrated recently during a staff conference. The intaker presented a case of a religious patient "who compulsively mumbled a prayer about holes and orifices after exiting from the lavatory." Several staff members opined that the patient was psychotic and recommended that he be given anti-psychotic medication until a more enlightened staff member explained that religious Jews recite a prayer after relieving themselves, thanking God for his wisdom in creating man.

In response to the above recommendation, a pilot program was recently initiated at Kaplan Hospital by the author and his colleagues, Drs. Nina Guy, Benjamin Feldman and Hannah Bar-Joseph. A prominent communal rabbi was invited to deliver a series of lectures to the mental health staff of the hospital (psychiatrists, psychologists, psychiatric social workers, psychiatric nurses, vocational and rehabilitation therapists and medical and psychology students training at the hospital) on "Mental Health and Judaism." Issues discussed including Judaism's view of and attitude towards the mentally ill, the halachic status of the mentally ill, the role of the rabbi in dealing with emotionally distressed and disturbed people, areas of conflict between rabbis and mental health practitioners, rabbis' attitude toward psychiatric and psychological treatment and cooperation between the two disciplines. These lectures were highly informative and produced spirited give and take between the speaker and the audience.

A series of ten lectures on various aspects of mental health was initiated by the above mental health practitioners for local clergymen. Topics included psychopathology, psychiatric and psychological treatment, re-habilitation and clergy-clinician cooperation. Twenty rabbis (who included mostly teachers and several community rabbis and Roshei Yeshivot) attended the lectures that were given by various mental health professionals (psychiatrists, psychologists, and social workers) from the hospital staff and other lecturers. The participants were asked to fill out a "feedback" questionnaire after each lecture and at the conclusion of the course.

The following is a summary of their responses:

To the question, "To what extent the course contributed to your understanding of the subject?", and "To what extent the course was important or interesting?" ninety-five percent of the respondents answered "very much." Seventy percent were of the opinion that the course helped them "very much" to clarify their position and attitude toward the subject, ninety percent were "very much" interested in additional lectures on the subject and one hundred percent stated that they would recommend that rabbis participate in similar courses. Sixty percent expressed the opinion that as a result of the course, they had a more positive attitude toward the subject of mental health and were more willing to refer people to mental health practitioners. Eighty percent were glad that the course was "for rabbis only" and were interested in participating in ongoing group consultation meetings with a mental health professional.

Rabbi Shlomo Wolbe, the late prominent haredi rabbi, author and educator wrote: "... there is an urgent need to organize courses for practicing rabbis and educators, in order to disseminate basic knowledge of the symptoms of neurosis and psychosis and their treatment, in order that they will know to refer mentally ill people immediately to the psychiatrist. Basic knowledge will remove many prejudices." (3)

It is highly recommended that religious mental health practitioners heed Rabbi Wolbe's call for the benefit of rabbis, clinicians, and the people they serve.

References

1. Greenberg, D. and Witztum,E. Editorial: "Ultra-orthodox Jewish attitudes toward mental health care". *Israel Journal of Psychiatry Related Sciences*, 31, no. 3 (1994): 143-44.

2. Lichner-Ingram, B. and Lowe, D.. "Counseling activities and referral practices of rabbis". Journal of Psychology and Judaism 13, no. 3 (1989): 133-48.

3. Wolbe, S. "Psychiatry and Religion" in "In the Pathways of Medicine," 5 Sivan, 5749. (Hebrew)

* * *

Comment by Professor Joshua H. Werblowsky, M. D., prominent orthodox Jewish psychiatrist:

The title of HaRav Sternbuch shlita teshuva 465 is "Is it correct to go to psychologists and psychiatrists to be healed?" The first line states "against going to them." HaRav Sternbuch does not differentiate between different kinds or religious levels of therapists in his teshuva.

It seems to me a teshuvah should answer the question asked in a manner that does not need further interpretation. There should be no need for extra commentary beyond what is written in the teshuvah.

If there were special circumstances HaRav Sternbuch was relating to, I feel they should have been included in the teshuvah. Contrast this teshuvah with that of HaRav Feinstein, zt"l Igros Moshe Yoreh Deah, 2:57 (paraphrased) The title "With regard to healing the mentally ill from a psychiatrist who is a heretic or atheist." HaRav Feinstein answered "In my opinion do not go to them...One should seek out a psychiatrist who is shomer Torah, and if none are available he should negotiate with the expert to promise not to discuss areas of belief and Torah."

There is specific validation in the teshuvah of HaRav Feinstein allowing for mental health treatment. Further, the teshuvah clarifies under what circumstances the treatment is permitted. I had the opportunity a number of years ago at a Yarchei Kallah to ask HaRav Sternbuch about his teshuvah to seek clarification. HaRav Sternbuch agreed that if an individual was threatening suicide one should go to a psychiatrist rather than a Rav. When asked if he differentiated between therapists based on their religious beliefs when he stated "against going to them," and if so why not include that information in his teshuva, he did not elaborate. In my opinion, it would be helpful if HaRav Sternbuch would write a teshuvah and elaborate under what circumstances and with whom mental health treatment would be acceptable.

What follows is a short comment with regard to Freudian psychological / psychiatric treatment: Freud described religion in The Future of an Illusion and other writings as an illusion, which of course we as Orthodox mental health professionals completely disagree with. However, with regard to actual therapy with patients, in short, his goal was "where id is there ego shall be." This means that unconscious drives should not prevail. Through therapy these drives should be mediated with healthy defense mechanisms, ego ideals and adaptive and executive functioning. Furthermore, psychoanalytic thinking has advanced beyond Freudian thought with focus on ego development, superego development, object relations theory and self-psychology. Psychoanalytic thought today has developed understanding of the meaning and importance of religion for clients and patients.

7

Brief Rabbinic Interventions in Psychological Treatment

In her study on orthodox rabbinic attitudes toward mental health professionals, Slanger (1996) makes the following points: "It is important for the mental health profession to assume responsibility for initiating contact with the rabbis and engaging in extensive case recruitment efforts"; "...it is essential to acknowledge areas of rabbinic expertise and to harmonize closely with the rabbis in a mutually working alliance"; "Therapeutic approaches which may include participation of the rabbis should be considered".

Below are presented five abbreviated case reports describing the collaborative efforts of rabbis and a clinical psychologist in the treatment of psychiatric patients where the outstanding elements were maladaptive behavior and reactions to extreme guilt feelings.

Case 1

Jonah, a 28 year old bachelor who several years ago became a "baal teshuva" (repentant), has lived in a hostel for discharged psychiatric patients for the last two years. During the past ten years he has been in psychiatric treatment, which included several hospitalizations. His diagnosis is, Schizophrenia, Unspecified Type and Obsessive-Compulsive Disorder, Mixed Obsessional Thoughts and Acts. He is presently receiving psychopharmacological and psychological treatment at a local mental health clinic.

Jonah was described by his therapist as a highly anxious, insecure, dependent, depressed, suspicious, immature, rigid and perseverative individual who was involved in a compulsive manner with issues of religion, dietary laws, cleanliness and food. These preoccupations severely encumbered his daily functioning, both vocationally and socially. His religious obsessional and compulsive preoccupations included excessive concern regarding observing the dietary laws (eg., dairy and meat products were compromised as a result of their being in close proximity to each other, etc.); concern that he inadvertently deleted several words from his prayer which prompted him to repeat the prayer and excessive concern regarding the cleanliness of his hands and body, especially before partaking of food and praying.

Jonah had approached several local rabbis about his religious questions and concerns who patiently explained to him the halacha (Jewish law) in an attempt to reassure and calm him. However, the intricate explanations only prompted more questions and doubts and increased his anxiety. At the request of the patient, the therapist arranged a meeting with a rabbi with whom he had collaborated in the past regarding religious patients in his care. Before the meeting, the psychologist met with the rabbi to discuss the strategic approach to be taken with the patient.

In the three-way meeting, the rabbi, after hearing the patient's questions and concerns for a half-hour, told the patient that because of his difficult emotional situation, he would be granted a special dispensation, and therefore, for him there were no questions and therefore no need for clarifications or explanations. As of today he did not have to worry if the food he eats has been compromised, and need not concern himself whether he skipped some words in his prayers or whether his body was adequately clean before doing a religious ritual. He was told to repeat this "mantra" — "There are no questions and therefore there is no need for answers". He was also informed that this special dispensation was in force for three months and to be renewed only after prior consultation between the rabbi and therapist. The rabbi wrote out his opinion, dated it, and gave it to the therapist to keep. At the conclusion of the session the rabbi wished the patient a speedy recovery and success in his endeavors.

In the following therapy session with the therapist, the patient reported a significant reduction in his religious obsessions. Whenever the patient attempted to raise religious concerns in the session, the therapist reminded him of the "mantra" and the discussion was refocused on other non-religious issues. Several years later, the patient's present therapist reported that the patient continues to use this "mantra" when plagued by religious obsessions, with partial success.

Case 2

Joseph is a 50 year old haredi (ultra-orthodox) man who three years ago married a divorcee with two children. He has three children from his first marriage whom he sees at rare occasions. For the last ten years he has run a large haredi school in Jerusalem with considerable success.

In the first meeting, he informed the therapist that he is a closed person, doesn't have many friends, doesn't trust people including his wife, and that he will not reveal personal information to the therapist. When asked about his marriage he responded that it was fine, his wife was a good woman and he took all the blame for all the difficulties between them. When pressed, he acknowledged that he feels like a guest in his home, he has no say regarding the discipline of his wife's children and because of his generosity with money (buys presents for his children and their mother), the bank account is in his wife's name. He doesn't have his own cellphone because his wife objects that he speaks to his former wife.

When asked why he decided to go for psychological treatment, he explained that he is not living a meaningful and productive life, lacks desire and energy to cope with life's everyday problems, and feels depressed and pessimistic about the future. When the therapist commented that it was understandable in light of his marital situation, Joseph insisted that he was to blame and that he had to work on him self to accept the situation for the sake of "shalom bayit" (domestic peace). He added that he had to work on his "middot" (attributes), "bitul hayesh" ("annihilation of the self") and learn to accept his situation with grace and tolerance. He denied that he harbored any angry feelings towards his wife and added that angry feelings are prohibited by halacha . Upon inquiry, he acknowledged that angry feelings were unacceptable in his house since he can remember. When asked if he discussed the above mentioned halachic-philosophical issues with a rabbi, he answered in the negative and explained that there wasn't any rabbi that he respected and trusted enough to confide in. At this point, the patient enquired if the therapist would arrange a meeting with a rabbi that the latter respected and trusted in order to discuss these issues.

At the following session (fifth), the rabbi met with Joseph together with the therapist at the latter's office and related to the halachic-philosophical issues raised by the patient. The rabbi opined that the patient's understanding and interpretation of the hassidic concept "bitul hayesh" was inaccurate as it had to be balanced and not create negative consequences. He also took issue regarding the patient's understanding of the halacha's view of anger. According to Rabbi Kook, the rabbi explained, when anger is a mode of life or when it is unjustified, it is prohibited. When a person is wronged, he is permitted to express his natural feelings. At this point the psychologist turned to the rabbi and stated that in his opinion Joseph was hiding behind a "halachic-philosophical smokescreen" in order to avoid acknowledging and dealing with his pent-up angry feelings and fears of behaving in an honest , forthright and assertive manner. He believes that by acting as a "doormat", he is acting in a righteous manner. The rabbi turned to the patient and encouraged him to start taking small steps toward assertiveness and suggested that the next meeting that he schedules with the therapist be done with his new cellphone, even though he may jeopardize "shalom bayit". Joseph unexpectedly responded that if the rabbi rules such, he will do it.

Several days later, Joseph called for an appointment with his new cellphone. At the meeting, Joseph seemed more relaxed and in a positive mood. He reported that he is more assertive at home and was surprised that he met less resistance from his wife than expected. At the end of the session, he mentioned that the previous meeting with the rabbi was very helpful and asked the therapist to again thank the latter for his help.

Case 3

David, a 29-year-old single man from a religious Iraqi family, is the youngest of six children and the only one who had not completed a high school education. At the age of 19 he was hospitalized with a diagnosis of chronic paranoid schizophrenia. In the past, David had worked in the post office and in sheltered workshops. He is presently involved in a rehabilitation program that involves occupational and social therapy and individual supportive therapy. In one of the therapy sessions, David raised the issue of masturbation. On the one hand he felt extreme conflict and guilt indulging in this behavior; on the other hand, he had no other avenue to release his strong sexual impulses. The guilt caused him considerable distress, depression and preoccupation with thoughts of punishment and suicide. The therapist suggested to David to discuss this issue with a rabbi and after receiving his consent, a meeting was arranged with a rabbi with wide experience in pastoral counseling.

After listening to the patient explain his conflict and dilemma, the rabbi, using appropriate halachic texts, counseled the patient to attempt to control his masturbatory activity since it was against Jewish law. He pointed out, however, that it was not possible to judge him since others could not know what he is feeling and experiencing. Because of his serious psychological problems he could be considered an *anoos (legal term for a person who has limited or no self-control and free choice regarding his behavior)* by society and especially, by his family. The rabbi added that David knew himself best; if he tried to control his behavior and did not succeed, it was an indication that he is an *anoos*. Therefore, there is no reason for guilt feelings. David mentioned to the rabbi that several years ago he had consulted a rabbi about the same issue and was told that his behavior was terrible and sinful, and that if he continued, an accident would befall him. The rabbi pointed out to the patient that since the dire predicted consequences did not occur, it proved that he might be considered an *anoos*. The rabbi terminated the meeting with a quote from the Talmudic text, "Ethics of the Fathers": "You are not called upon to complete the work, yet you are not free to evade it". A week later, the therapist contacted the rabbi and informed him that following the meeting there was a noticeable improvement in the patient's mood and general functioning and thanked him for his help.

Case 4

Dinah, a thirty year old married woman and mother of three children requested an immediate appointment as she was afraid that out of desperation, she will do harm to herself. The patient appeared tense and anxious as she described her fragile emotional state. For the last two years, after a religious friend of hers in whom she confided, told her that in the Talmud it states that the punishment for not keeping vows is the premature death of children, she has been obsessed with guilt feelings, fears and thoughts of making vows and receiving divine punishment for not fulfilling them. Her emotional stability has been further aggravated as a result of marital tension and conflict.

Following the initial session, Dinah felt less anxious and tense and in more control of her emotions. In the fourth meeting when she again raised the issue of her obsessional thoughts and fears, the therapist suggested a meeting with a religious authority in order to discuss further this issue, to which the patient enthusiastically agreed.

In discussing the case with the rabbi, the therapist suggested that the former arrange a religious ceremony of "Hatarat Nedarim", (Annulment of Vows) * as a means of aiding the patient to free herself from the oppressive bonds of her obsessional fears.

The meeting was held in the rabbi's synagogue and was attended by the therapist and another man. The rabbi, after listening to the patient's story, explained that it is a sin to make vows and not fulfill them but thoughts of making vows are not prohibited. The Torah, however, realized that man is only human and is not capable of controlling all the time his speech and, therefore, provided a way to annul vows that were made impulsively and now regretted. After explaining the form and purpose of the above mentioned religious ritual, the rabbi conducted the ceremony with the participation of two other men. At the conclusion of the meeting, the patient, visibly relieved, thanked the rabbi for his help. The latter wrote out what transpired at the meeting, signed the note and asked the other two participants to do likewise and handed it to the patient for future reference.

---

* It is considered a fearsome sin for one to violate vows and oaths ("He shall not desecrate his word"-Numbers, 30:3) and the mainstream rabbinic view was against making vows in general ("Do not form the habit of making vows"-Babylonian Talmud, Nedarimm, 20,a). However, Jewish law provides the possibility of annulment of vows if the vow involves only oneself. One remedy is the ceremony of "Hatarat Nedarim", recited on the eve of Rosh Hashana, the Jewish New Year. In this ceremony, three individuals band together and take turns in constituting a quasi-ecclesiastical court. The petitioner recites a formula whereby he renounces all oaths and promises made and not fulfilled. He expresses regret in taking upon himself vows and requests that they be annulled. The "judges" then declare that there "do not exist any vows"... "but there does exist pardon, forgiveness and atonement". The ceremony is concluded with the petitioner declaring for the final time that "he cancels from this time onward all vows and all oaths". The ceremony is declared proactive so that if an oath is made subsequently and then regretted, it too is declared totally null and void. (Rapaport, 1991)

In the following therapy session, the patient reported a marked decrease in her obsessional thoughts and a significant improvement in her mood and overall functioning.

Case 5

Dan, a 25 year old bachelor who immigrated to Israel with his mother and older sister five years ago, appeared at the clinic with the following complaints: severe depression, poor concentration, pains in the chest and legs, decreased functioning at work, and an overpowering feeling that he was "going crazy" from his constant thoughts regarding the death of his father. Though he had suffered for the last ten years, he refused to seek psychiatric aid until his mother pleaded with him to do so.

His father, who suffered from several serious physical illnesses and who had a long psychiatric history, expressed a desire to end his life. One day the patient found him attempting to hang himself from a basement rafter. The father asked the son to move the table upon which he was standing so that he could die, but the son refused. After repeated taunting and pleading the son in an attempt to appease his father, moved the table from under his father's feet and immediately returned it to its original place. The father, enraged at his son's action, began cursing and yelling at him to move the table. The son again moved the table, but this time was unsuccessful in returning it to its original place because of the father's frantic kicking movements. The patient immediately ran to his mother for help, but on their return, the father had already expired.

A year before seeking psychiatric help, the patient established a relationship with a woman, with whom he was presently sharing an apartment, but not his "awful secret." The patient felt that he could not marry and bring children into the world because of his fear of not being able to function as a husband and father and "going crazy."

In the therapy sessions, an attempt was made to relate to and deal with the patient's intense and overwhelming guilt feelings regarding the "patricidal" act and his self-punishing behavior, but with little success. At one point, the therapist suggested consulting a rabbi regarding the possibility of atonement for the patient. The patient, who came from a traditional background, agreed. However, he requested that the therapist speak to the rabbi first, in order to prepare him for the "shocking" story. In the meeting with the rabbi, the psychologist presented briefly the patient's history and the purpose and goals of the upcoming meeting.

The meeting with the patient was held in a synagogue in the presence of the psychologist. After hearing the patient's story, the rabbi stated that the offense committed was indeed very serious. He proceeded to explicate on Judaism's view of the sanctity of life and then read several select portions from Maimonides on repentance. The rabbi then concluded:

"According to the Torah, you are obligated to believe that nothing stands in the way of repentance and this includes even the serious offence that you committed. I am also not convinced that all the responsibility falls upon you, in view of your father's erratic condition and disturbed behavior. The Torah requires that the penitent go through a process of experiencing and suffering guilt feelings and regret for the offense committed, a process that you have undergone more than is required and it is a pity that it has continued for so long. You are now required to pass on to the second stage of identity change* and doing good and charitable deeds.

---

* Part of the therapeutic process in cases of Post-Traumatic Stress Disorder of "accident killers" is "to forgive themselves and move on to redefinition and acceptance of the self". See, Janoff-Bulman, Shattered Assumptions: Towards a New Psychology of Trauma, 1992, New York: The Free Press.

It seems to me that you can realize identity change by getting married and having children. By naming your child after your deceased father, you will be perpetuating his memory for generations. You should also take upon yourself to donate money to a worthwhile charity in your father's name, visit his grave and in the presence of family members pronounce the new path that you have taken upon yourself and say the Kaddish (prayer recited by the mourner over the death of a close relative). God's mercy will never cease and may he provide you with a complete recovery and forgive your sins."

The patient was given the written opinion of the rabbi as he had requested and instructed to take it home to study. He was told it might take him a while to digest the significance of the meeting and the content of the letter and that he should contact the therapist when he felt ready for a meeting. A half-year later, the patient's girlfriend telephoned to invite the therapist to their wedding and requested that he ask the rabbi to officiate as he had offered in his initial meeting with the patient. In response to the therapist's inquiry, she reported that her fiancé was doing well and there was a significant decrease in his somatic complaints. The meeting and letter of the rabbi had a profound influence on him, as it forced him to face reality. She mentioned that several weeks ago, he had visited his father's grave, where he had announced his intention to marry and asked his father for his blessing. A week before the wedding, the couple had a premarital consultation meeting with the rabbi and the following day Dan donated several volumes of religious books, including the writings of Maimonides, to the synagogue, in his father's memory.

Conclusion

In the above cases, the rabbis' role and interventions aided the patients to extricate themselves from the guilt-ridden quicksand which imprisoned them. The result was a considerable remission in their suffering and symptoms and a freeing of their energies and thoughts toward change and growth.

While the psychotherapist can explore the subject of guilt, morality, conscience, etc., he cannot participate with the guilty person in repentance, confession, and atonement or offer dispensations. Here, only that person whom the "guilty" man "acknowledges as a hearer and speaker who represents the transcendence believed in by the 'guilty' man, can speak." (Buber, 1965)

References

Buber, M., Guilt and guilt feelings, In: Friedman, M., Ed., The Knowledge of Man. New York: Harper Torchbooks, 1965.

Rapaport, , J. L., The Boy Who Couldn't Stop Washing. New York: Signet, 1991, (pp. 176-191).

Slanger, C., Orthodox rabbinic attitudes to mental health professionals and referral patterns. Tradition, 31, 1, 22-33, 1996.

8

*Religious Issues
in Psychological Treatment:
Contemporary Responsa*

There is a dearth of halachic literature that deals with psychotherapy issues which is in sharp contrast to medical issues. One explanation could be that religious therapists view rabbis as unsympathetic if not hostile toward their profession and psychology in general and that Torah views are viewed as frequently inconsistent with the views of their profession and therefore are threatened by their possible interventions. Therefore, if there are no questions, one cannot expect much response in this area.

Below are interesting and relevant questions raised by religious practitioners of psychotherapy, responses of prominent contemporary orthodox rabbis and comments by the author.

Psychotherapy and Honoring Parents

Rabbi Yitzchok Zilberstein, a respected halachic authority, was asked the following question by a psychologist: "If during a psychological evaluation, the psychologist forms the opinion that the child's problems are related to the detrimental relationship with his parents because of his and/or their problems, is it permissible for the psychologist to bring this to the child's attention?" The rabbi's response (which appeared in "Assia," 2-43, 11,2-3, Nison, 5747) was:

"It is prohibited to make the child aware of the contribution of his parents to his problems lest he cause him to transgress, 'Cursed be he that dishonors his father and mother' (Deuteronomy, 26, 16) and one does not cure through transgressions."

This rabbinic ruling prompted the author to present to Rabbi Zilberstein the following brief case study preceded by a short introduction.

A considerable number of difficulties, problems and psychopathology of children (and adults who are stuck in their childhood) are a result of parental "misbehavior" (double messages, exploitations, excessive demands, criticism and expectations, involvement of their child in parental conflicts, engenderment of excessive guilt feelings, etc.)

In psychological treatment the therapist attempts to aid the child (adult) to understand, recognize and identify his inner conflicts, fears, anxieties, ambivalent feelings and the troublesome and pathological behavior that stems from them and help him develop more effective and appropriate ways to cope with his internal conflicts and life's stresses and demands.

In individual, family and group therapy, the therapist at times may encourage the patient, directly or indirectly, to externalize and express his pent up angry feelings toward the significant people in his life — his boss, spouse, sibling or parent, rather than suppress and internalize them, since this can result in the development of somatic symptoms, excessive guilt and self punishment and a distorted negative self image.

Question: Are the above therapeutic interventions permissible since this may cause the patient to transgress, "Cursed be he that dishonors his father and mother".

To explicate the question, a brief case study in presented:

An 18-year-old university coed applied to the counseling service because of severe depression, intense social anxiety and difficulty in concentration in her studies. This was done without her parent's knowledge for fear that they would punish her.

In the third session, the patient, with great hesitancy and anguish, revealed to her therapist that, from the age of ten, her father has been sexually abusing her. Against her will, he had touched the intimate parts of her body, kissed her on the lips and insisted that the door to her bedroom be ajar and the door of the shower room unlocked when she bathed.

The patient slept uneasily at night and showered while wearing her undergarments for fear of an expected visit from her father. The patient did not *protest* for fear of being totally rejected and/or punished by her father. She did not tell her mother because the latter was weak and always sided with her husband. The patient felt that she was in some way responsible for her father's behavior and attempted to diminish her "femininity" by losing a great deal of weight, thus endangering her health. She viewed herself as a wicked person who deserved punishment and frequently inflicted upon herself bodily harm in order to "atone for her sins." She had frequently entertained suicidal thoughts but never attempted to end her life.

The goals of therapy were to help the patient view herself as a victim and not as a partner to sinful behavior, to give legitimacy to her pent-up anger toward her father, encourage her to externalize rather than internalize her feelings and stand up and repudiate her father's inappropriate, non-paternal behavior.

Gradually, the patient became more assertive and repelled her father's advances and insisted that her bedroom door be closed and the shower room door be locked when she bathed. In the therapy sessions, she permitted herself to speak more freely about her fear and hatred of her father and her anger and disappointment in her mother. The patient started to gain weight, dress in an appropriate feminine fashion and increase her social contacts. Her self-image improved as well as her concentration and academic work. A year after termination of therapy, the patient married and graduated from the university with high marks.

From a halachic perspective did the therapist fulfill the following commandments?

1. "Cause him to be thoroughly healed" (Exodus, 21, 19);
2. "Return it to him" (Exodus, 23, 4); ie., mental health: and "Neither shall thou stand idly by the blood of thy neighbor" (Leviticus, 19, 16), for one can view the father, in this case, as a pursuer" who is endangering the mental health and well being of his daughter, or did he unwittingly cause the patient to transgress "Cursed be he that dishonors his father and mother"?

Rabbi Zilberstein's response:

One has to divide the answer into two parts:
1. In a situation where the father has not repented and continues in his wicked ways.
2. Where the father has repented.

Regarding the first situation, it is stated in the Shulchan Aruch (standard book of Jewish law), Yoreh Deah, chapter 240, paragraph 18 in the glosses or the Rama, "Some say that as long as the father did not repent, there is no obligation to honor him."

In light of this opinion, there is no question since there is no obligation to honor a wicked father. However, this is not so simple since the Schach comments there (ibid, subparagraph 20), "Even though there is no obligation to honor him, it is prohibited to distress him". Note it.

In light of this, if the father discovers that his daughter is receiving psychological treatment and is being encouraged and directed to vent her negative feelings toward him, he will be distressed, and this is prohibited.

It could be that even if the father does find out that his daughter is receiving psychological treatment, it is permissible, for the prohibition to demean and disrespect him is only when the aim is for the sake of denigration but not when it is done for therapeutic purposes and for the benefit of his daughter which in the end is for his benefit also, so that he will have a healthy daughter, suitable for marriage and the continuation of his progeny and this is not "embarrassment" but "rehabilitation" and preparation for marriage. And proof that it is permitted to shame and distress the father for desirable benefits is derived from King Hezekiah who dragged his father's bones on a bed of sackcloth as is explained in the tractate Pesachim, 56. Rashi explained there that he dragged his father's bones for his atonement and did not bury him in kingly splendor, for the sanctification of God, that he be censured for his wickedness and his wicked deeds be removed.

The tractate concludes that the sages acknowledged that he acted correctly. Therefore, it is permitted to humiliate a father for a benefit and especially when the father destroyed his daughter's world, he is obligated to suffer in order that she be cured.

And if the father repented, one can assume that he prefers that his daughter despise him in her heart in order that she can marry and that this will be his atonement for what he did to her and maybe it is proper to involve and consult the father regarding the therapeutic process in order to prevent as much as possible his embarrassment.

And after the daughter is cured and her wounds are healed, it is proper to urge her to return to respect her father for she is obligated to him for bringing her into the world and in spite of the damage that he inflicted on her, her debt to her father has not expired.

In summary, the above treatment is permissible and the psychologist fulfilled the aforementioned commandments.

Psychologist comments:

It appears that the rabbi's lenient ruling applies only to parents who are viewed halachically as "wicked" and therefore their permission for their children to receive psychological treatment (where they are free to express their negative feelings toward their "wicked" parents) is not required. It is not clear whether chi!dren (youngster and adults) of "non-wicked" parents are permitted to receive psychological treatment against the wishes of their parents (who unintentionally have and are presently causing psychological problems and emotional difficulties to their children — see introductory remarks) who either deny that their children have emotional and behavioral problems, don't believe in psychological treatment or are embarrassed that other people know of their problems and conflicts.

Is the prohibition, "Cursed be he that dishonors his father and mother" inapplicable to treatment situations where the goals are healing and rehabilitation, or does the honor of parents take precedence over the aforementioned goals?

The above question has relevance not only to the religious therapist but also to the religious patient who may be hesitant and reluctant to discuss his problems, conflicts and feelings openly for fear of transgressing a biblical prohibition.

Rabbi Zilberstein's response:

If the father is not "wicked," one is not permitted to go against his wishes regarding his declination of psychological treatment (for his child), unless by rabbinic decree. And if this is brought before a rabbi and he is of the opinion that it is in the best interest of the child to receive psychological treatment, the father has no authority to dispute with the rabbi. The judgment of a rabbi is similar to that of a court and it is a commandment to listen to the words of the sages. If the father does not fulfill his commandment, there is no obligation to honor him. Even if the rabbi instructs the father to permit his child to speak about him, this is not disparagement but a form of healing. Furthermore, the father also bears some guilt in that he caused this situation. Therefore, there is no slighting of his honor, rather healing and rehabilitation of the child.

* * *

Comments by Rabbi Naftali Bar-Ilan, Communal Rabbi of Rehovot, Israel.

Regarding the article on "Psychotherapy and Honoring Parents", the most important lesson we can learn from this article is that one should not present general questions to a rabbi (and that the rabbi should not respond to general questions) but provide specific, relevant and pertinent information so that the rabbi can direct his response to the specific person and situation.

Secondly, Rabbi Zilberstein is of the opinion that there are situations that one should turn to a mental health expert for help and that psychological treatment can be permissible according to halacha, even if it involves offending the honor of parents. However, one should be careful not to offend the honor of parents when it is not vital to the treatment. Therefore, this kind of treatment is permissible only when it is vital to treatment, there is the possibility that it will succeed, and that the offending behavior towards the parents will not exceed that which is required for the treatment to succeed.

The halachic ruling regarding psychological treatment is similar to halachic rulings regarding medical treatments that involve halachic prohibitions. For example, in a situation where an abortion is being contemplated, the physician should provide the pertinent information to a rabbi and he will decide according to halacha, whether to permit performing the abortion.

Rabbi Nachum Rabinovitch, Rosh Yeshiva, Birkat Moshe, Maaleh Adumim was presented with the following question.

A middle-aged religious mother of five children mentioned in the initial therapy session that her husband was physically abusive to her and her children, as was her father toward her and her mother. "My father was a terrible person. Am I allowed to say that?"

What is the halachic position regarding children (young or adult) speaking disparagingly and expressing anger and hate toward their parents in the therapy session (individual, family, group)? Is it permissible since the purpose and goal are healing and rehabilitation of the tormented and dysfunctional patient, or prohibited because of the biblical injunction, "Cursed be he that dishonors his father and mother"?

Rabbi Rabinovitch's response:

If the expression of negative feelings is intended to bring about a therapeutic result, it is certainly justified.

On the other hand, one must always bear in mind that real or imaginary hurts are sometimes exaggerated far out of proportion. It would seem to me that part of the therapist's task is to help the patient see things in their proper perspective, and thus to enable pent-up feeling to be released in a controlled manner. Even a child needs to learn to see the total picture, even when it is necessary to "bad mouth" certain aspects of it.

Therapist Obligation to Report Transgressions

The following question was presented to Rabbi Nachum Rabinovitch, Rosh Yeshivah of Birkat Moshe in Maaleh Adumim:

A woman confided to her psychologist in a treatment session that she had not been attending the mikveh (ritualarium) for the last several months and doesn't plan to in the future, without the knowledge of her husband. Is the therapist obligated to betray professional confidence and inform her husband that his wife is causing him to transgress a biblical prohibition? Does the biblical prohibition "Thou shall not stand idly by the blood of thy neighbor" (Leviticus 19:16) apply in this situation?

On the other hand, betraying professional confidence will possibly
1. cause the client to discontinue vital psychological treatment;
2. discourage other people who are in need of psychological treatment

from going to religious psychotherapists; 3. significantly reduce potential referrals, and thereby, the therapist's income.

Rabbi Rabinovitch's response:

I wonder whether a patient's statement to her therapist is necessarily credible. Even if there were no doubt at all about its truth, it still would not have the status of certain knowledge for the therapist, and especially in view of the fact that patients are known to invent tales in fulfillment of desires of one kind or another.

In any case, it seems to me that a religious therapist is duty-bound to find ways to try to convince his patient not to transgress. I realize that some psychologists are opposed to a judgmental stance, but such opposition seems to me to be against Torah law.

Comment

A psychotherapist is obligated and has an unwritten contract with his client to help him cope more effectively with problems, conflicts, and issues that are of concern to him and which are causing him distress and difficulty in his everyday functioning and not issues that are of concern to the religious practitioner. Furthermore, raising (no matter how sensitively) religious and moral issues (such as mikveh and abortion), which are issues of no concern to the non-committed client, will, in all probability, cause the patient to flee from vital psychological treatment, as he/she will interpret the therapist's behavior as "missionary" and not therapeutic.

Rabbi Zilberstein, a highly respected authority on Jewish law ruled, "It is clear that the therapist is obligated to inform her husband."

In his article "Privacy: A Jewish Perspective" in the Journal of Halacha and Contemporary Society, vol. 82 (1981), Rabbi Alfred Cohen wrote:

A person whose livelihood depends upon maintaining the confidentiality of revelations made to him need not jeopardize his position by telling those secrets. Although keeping silent might violate the negative mitzvah (commandment) of not standing by and allowing another Jew to be harmed, yet as long as he is not violating the mitzvah of *doing* any action, and taking action would endanger his own livelihood, then he is permitted to remain silent...

Even if there would be no monetary loss involved for the counselor, yet there remains the question whether professional counseling could continue as a viable activity if the public could not rely upon absolute inviolability of confidence...

Obviously, fear of exposure would preclude many persons from seeking help they desperately need...

Is it beneficial for the community to have available to it people with skill and knowledge to help those in pain and confusion? I think yes, very much so. Can we allow this benefit to the community to take precedence over the rights and prerogatives of the individuals within the community? The preponderance of rabbinical opinion in this area leads clearly to the conclusion that the public needs override the personal welfare of the individual.

See also: *Assia* 1 (5746) "Sodiut Refuiyut Mul Interes Tsibur, Emek Halakhah," 149-157, 154 (in Hebrew).

Counselling a Kohen Married to a Divorcée

The following question was sent to the Schlesinger Institute International Responsa Project:

Can a marriage counselor continue to treat a couple after he learns that the husband is a kohen [member of the priestly class] and the wife is a divorcée [prohibited to a kohen]?

Rabbi David Kaye, who chairs the medical ethics department of the Parker Jewish Institute for Health Care and Rehabilitation, responded:

> Absolutely not! The Torah clearly and explicitly prohibits a kohen from marrying several types of women, one of whom is a grushah (divorcée).Part of the biblical imperative of v'kidashto (and you shall sanctify him) is that a kohen may not choose to forgo his sanctity and marry such a woman.
>
> Furthermore, the Talmud (Yevamot 88b) understands that there is an affirmative imperative upon others to see to it that a kohen maintains his sanctified status—v'kidashto bal korho. Rashi (on Leviticus 21:8) thus says that a kohen who refuses to divorce his prohibited wife is to be whipped until he complies. (See also Rivash responsum 348, Be'er Moshe responsum 5:159.) There is no question that a Torah-observant therapist has the same obligation as any other Jew and must do what he/she can to separate the couple.
>
> However, as a marriage therapist there may be cogent reasons (licensure reasons, malpractice concerns) not to do so. But it is clear that the therapist cannot continue to counsel and assist the couple. While there may be "professional" reasons not to take affirmative steps to "split them up," the therapist must explain to the clients that he/she can no longer assist them in solving their marital problems/issues since they are in a prohibited relationship. This is no different from other situations in which a therapist discovers conflicts and must end the therapeutic relationship. Also, continuing to counsel the couple would violate the prohibition against placing a stumbling block before the blind... (See Radvaz responsum 187.)

Rabbi Shabtai Rappoport, Rosh Yeshivah Shvut Yisrael and Beit Hamedrash, Machon Hagavoha L'Torah, Bar-Ilan University response to the above question:

The question you raise should be examined from two aspects: the obligation of a non-professional person in these circumstances, and the differences, if any, between a non-professional and a professional. A non-professional is obligated by the mitsvah of tokhehah (rebuke) to convince a kohen to divorce his forbidden wife. In case it proves impossible, one must not show support to such a couple. Showing such support is a transgression against the prohibition of aiding a transgression, as explained by Rabbi Moshe Feinstein (Igrot Moshe, vol. 5, Orah Hayyim, part 5, siman 13, paragraph 7). The person supporting the transgressors becomes a sort of accessory, whereas all members of the Jewish public should abhor and show their abhorrence of the transgression of any commandment. Here, though, a professional differs. In my opinion, the professional is bound to the command to rebuke transgressors only in relevant ways. He should endeavor to show the couple that marriage against our Torah could not come to a good end—as he should firmly and honestly believe.

However, when tokhehah is not possible, his relationship with the couple is not social, and hence he does not relate to them as a member of the Jewish community. In the professional context, accepting a situation as a given baseline does not constitute a personal opinion, and thus it does not seem as if the professional condones the patient's behavior. A professional who treats a child abuser does not express his opinion regarding this abuse. That is why he is not considered as aiding transgression. (Igrot Moshe, ibid.)

Therapist Being Alone with a Patient of the Opposite Sex (Yichud)

Rabbi Gedalia Schwartz, the Av Beit Din (head of the rabbinical court) of the Rabbinical Council of America stated that the principle of osek be'melakhto (a person working in his profession) and the fact that sexual boundary violations are grounds for losing one's license are important mitigating factors. His opinion is that closed doors that are unlocked, even if it is highly unlikely and only theoretically possible for someone to interrupt the session, do not pose a yihud problem. (My thanks to Dr. Nachum Klafter for bringing this halachic decision to my attention).

Addenda

9

"Therapist Friendly" and "Therapist Unfriendly" Attitudes and Views of Psychotherapy

"Therapist-Unfriendly":

In addition to the negative and hostile comments of prominent haredi rabbis to psychotherapy mentioned in the first chapter, one can add the following:

In "Binat Hamidot", (Feldheim, 2007), which contains a collection of writings by prominent haredi rabbis published by a haredi organization, Binat Halev, one can find many more examples of "therapist/psychology-unfriendly" statements and views.For example (page 12):

Question:If a young boy suffers from severe inferiority feelings and feels that he is unable to do anything, is this also midot? Answer: Certainly. Inferiority feelings are pride. If one is haughty, he thinks that he should be something better and no one recognizes it. This is what pains him. And if he knew what is the truth, it would not pain him. It only pains him because he thinks that he is great and does not accept what he has to accept. Everything is midot.

Page 81: When a person complains that his actions are a result of compulsiveness, that he is not able to abstain from this, we have to explain to him the simple truth that a Bet Din would have flogged him ...therefore our obligations as therapists are to shame him...this is what will arouse his self-esteem which is his inner existence, and will help him to accept upon himself responsibility for his actions and behave as a sensible person.

Rabbi Eliezer Melamed, Rosh Yeshiva, Har Bracha, commented in the weekly "Arutz-7 (27. 1. 05), in his article, "Psychologists and Honoring Parents": "Problem of Psychologists":

Many psychologists nowadays tend to blame a patient's problems on his parents;* they pressured him, got angry at him, and even hit him. In other words, "abused" him. Since the patient is considered a victim of his parent's treatment, it follows that he himself is never to blame for his troubles. His conscience can be clear and he can free himself from his distress. The parents are to blame for all his problems and troubles which he inflicts upon himself and his surroundings.

From this perspective, it is clear that the relationship between the child and parents will worsen and with the encouragement of the psychologist, he will scornfully transgress the commandment of honoring parents. Even if such a treatment would have been psychologically effective, it is nevertheless forbidden to take part in it since it is against the laws of the Torah. Just as a person is not allowed to steal or murder in order to relieve himself of suffering, so he may not transgress the commandment of respecting his parents in order to relieve himself of suffering.

*Comments by author:

Torah sources are also "guilty" of this. See I *Kings* 1:6.

Also see Rabbi Samson Raphael Hirsch's comment on the verse "When the boys grew up..." (Genesis 25:27) that the Talmud Sages point out that "the striking contrast in the grandchildren of Abraham may have been due not so much to a difference in their temperaments, as to mistakes in the way they were brought up. The great principle 'Bring up each child in accordance with his own way' was forgotten."

Rabbi Yaakov Kanievksy states in *Orhot Yosher*, p. 14 that "if the father and mother are not identical in their speech; one says right and one says left, and the son sees quarrels, then he is not executed as a 'stubborn and rebellious son' son, since his parents are at fault and not him."

Dr. Ben Zion Sorotzkin brought to my attention the following enlightening anecdote from *Sefer Binat Hamidot* (Jerusalem: Feldheim, 2007, in Hebrew) Introduction, p. 10:

> A yeshivah student was caught a number of times desecrating the Sabbath in the dormitory.
>
> The deans of the yeshivah went to their mentor Rabbi Elazar Menahem Man Shach to obtain his approval to expel the boy from the yeshivah. Rabbi Shach was very weak and frail in his advanced age. "What is the financial situation at home? How is his parents' marriage?" he asked.
>
> The deans were surprised by these questions. "How should we know what is happening in his house?" they asked.
>
> Rabbi Shach became visibly agitated and with great difficulty, he pushed himself up on the table to his full height, and with tears streaming down his face, he yelled at them "Rodfim, gei avek phun mayn shtub!! ["Murder-minded pursuers, get out of my house!!]. I don't want to speak to you. You don't know the home situation, You don't delve into his personal life. All you know is to throw him into the street!!"
>
> The staff hurried to investigate and discovered that the family suffered from extreme poverty and the parents had just recently divorced.

In a posthumous book of Rabbi Wolbe's letters and writings in a letter dated 12 Tishrei 5747, Rabbi Wolbe wrote: "In my work with people I see more and more the destruction that psychology causes us…I reached the conclusion that we have to eject psychology from our community as much as possible… But every Monday and Thursday students come to me and complain that they lack self-confidence, and I ask them, "Where is it written in the Torah that one needs self-confidence, and that it is something good? In the books I find that only confidence in G-d is necessary." *Igarot V'Katavim, Ha'Rav Shlomo Wolbe* (Jerusalem: Ha'Vaad L'Hotsaat Kitvey Ha'Mashgiah, 5765) p. 48.

* * *

"Therapist Friendly":

"Therapist friendly" views and comments by prominent haredi rabbis, amongst others:

Nahum Stepansky, Re'eh Ve'Aleyhu, Lo Yebol (Jerusalem: 5761) vol. 2, p. 134, article 147, wrote that the great adjudicator Rabbi Shlomo Zalman Auerbach is quoted as ruling "It is permitted to consult with a psychologist if it will help...So what if it is the wisdom of Gentiles? If there is good advice that can help, why not accept it."

In Yosef and Ruth Eliyahu, Ha'Torah Ha'Mesamahat (Beit El: 5758) p. 155, it is reported that after Rabbi Auerbach clarified with a psychologist what his treatment plans were, he decreed "Not only is the treatment permissible but it is a mitsvah."

In the weekly magazine "The Haredi Camp" (Machane Haredi) published by the Belz Hassidim (October 2008), appeared an interview with the well known educator and author, Rabbi Aharon Friedman:

Question: To what extent are psychologists involved in the treatment of haredi yeshiva students?

Answer: I do not have the required data to answer such a question. However, as far as I know, and I very much hope and believe that this is in fact the situation, there is a certain division of labor inside the Yeshiva. Regarding religious issues and those pertaining to character-improvement (middot), one seeks the advice of a wise, understanding Mashgiach (spiritual counselor), who is capable of conversing with the student and having a positive influence on him. Whereas, if there is a question of an emotional weakness or illness, regarding which the Mashgiach has no knowledge or experience, the right thing to do is to refer the student to professional assistance – just as one goes to a medical doctor in the case of bodily illness, or to a plumber.

Rabbi Shlomo Wolbe, z"l a prominent Israeli haredi rabbi, author and educator wrote in an article ("Psychiatry and Religion" in "In the Pathways of Medicine," 5 Sivan, 5749 (Hebrew)), "there is an urgent need to organize courses for practicing rabbis and educators, in order to disseminate basic knowledge of the symptoms of neurosis and psychosis and their treatment, in order that they will know to refer mentally ill people immediately to the psychiatrist. Basic knowledge will remove many prejudices."

In his book, "Aleinu Leshabeach" on "Numbers", page 171, Rabbi Yitchak Zilberstein relates a long story about how Rabbi Schach brought a student on Passover eve for treatment by a psychologist in Jerusalem and waited for him until the session ended to return him to his house.

In "Divrei Chachomim" (Rabbi Ginzberg, New York, 5,746), appeared the following question and answer.

Question: Today we find many Torah students that learn psychology and wish to be what is called "Torah Psychologists". Is there something like this in the Torah view since it appears that there are many things that are in contradiction with the views of Torah.

Answer: I heard from Rabbi Hanoch Leibowitz, zt"l, that in the past generations there was no need for all this, since the great sages had complete understanding of the wisdom of man, the patience and time to treat students that required this, and also, when they told them what to do, because they respected them greatly, they acceded to their advice, and all was well. However, today the great sages lack these things (and also respect for Torah is not as it was in previous generations), therefore there is today a need for this and only that they go in accordance with the Torah view and take from it only what can be of help (and not what that contradicts the Torah's view. (I also heard that Rabbi Feinstein agreed with this).

(I am indebted to Rabbi Naphtali Bar-Ilan for the above references and his helpful inputs and comments).

* * *

Whether psychotherapy as a discipline is seen as threatening or beneficial to Torah life may depend on whether psychotherapy is seen as a liberal philosophy based on secular values, or whether it is seen primarily as a form of treatment for psychological problems. Recently, a prominent Torah-observant psychiatrist and psychoanalyst, Dr. Nachum Klafter, articulated his understanding of how psychotherapy treatment should be conceptualized as separate from and therefore not conflicting with Torah beliefs and observance of halakhah.

Torah study and Torah observance are not treatments for psychopathology. They are the path given to us by G-d and our Sages to refine ourselves for the purpose of greater awareness of and service toward our Creator. Individuals suffering from personality disorders, mood disorders, severe anxiety disorders, psychotic disorders, and other significant psychopathology are impaired in their ability to serve G-d and study Torah. This may be because of straightforward cognitive limitations or behavioral problems. Or, more likely, it may be due to impaired ability to engage in meaningful interpersonal relationships. Relationship problems, in turn, severely impair a person's ability to take advice, benefit from spiritual direction, make friends, work or hold jobs, get married, provide effective parenting for their children, and participate in community responsibilities. Such patients will not benefit from a *mussar schmooze* (ethics talk) or a *humra* (strict interpretation). Such patients need *treatment*. After they have received successful treatment, they will be more capable of pursuing Torah and mitsvot, if they wish to. After they have received successful treatment, they will be more likely to benefit from mussar. In other words, their free choice is limited by their psychological difficulties. With successful treatment, their free choice is expanded. As a psychiatrist, psychotherapist, and psychoanalyst, it is not my role to bring Gentiles closer to the seven Noahide mitsvot or Jews to the 613 commandments. Enacting that role would sabotage my ability to help restore mental health. I am licensed as an expert in treating psychopathology. No matter how great a scholar I might be, I am not licensed to teach Torah or bring back stray souls. For example, I am currently treating a young woman who is afraid that she will not be able to consummate her marriage with her fiancé. She is afraid of being pushed around, disrespected, humiliated, dominated, and rejected… As we work through the conflicts embedded in her fantasies, she is becoming less fearful of intimacy. Torah study and mitsvot are of no help to her with these problems. She has her problems despite being a sincerely religious woman. Countless religious mentors have offered her advice. None of it has helped because Torah and mitsvot are not mental health treatments…Torah study and strict adherence to the halakhah does not automatically protect us from leading lives that are unbalanced, unhappy, and unfulfilled.

10

Ultra-Orthodox Rabbinic Responses to Religious Obsessive-Compulsive Disorder

David Greenberg, M. D. and Gaby Shefler, Ph. D.

Abstract: This presentation deals with the response of rabbis to ultra-orthodox people suffering from religious symptoms of obsessive-compulsive disorder. The symptoms are consistent with religious practice and patients justify their compulsive behaviors by the dictates of the codes of law. Will rabbis see their primary role as protection of the codes of law rather than alleviation of the suffering of the faithful? Will they see the person as someone who is meritoriously meticulous or in need of help? The writings of two eminent rabbis, and advice related by contemporary patients in Jerusalem, Israel are presented. The most arresting example of guidance is provided by Rabbi Nahman of Bratslav (1772–1810) who declared that he himself suffered from excessive religious practices typical of religious OCD until he overcame them. The accounts of rabbis and patients have features similar to the cognitive-behavioral treatment of choice for this disorder. The guidance of a rabbi is based on authority, and detailed knowledge of religious law, while a mental health therapist is an expert on OCD. The latter cannot give religious guidance, and has no authority within the ultra-orthodox community, and is only afforded a role with the rabbi's acquiescence. The role of the patient's rabbi is likely to be crucial in management. Religious guidance without professional help may often only have short-term benefit in this generally chronic condition, although studies have not been carried out.

Introduction

Tension between psychotherapy and religious authority is not new. In all religions, there are people whose role includes giving guidance and relief. Frank described the similarities between religious healing and psychotherapy (1), while Fromm and others saw the role of the psychoanalyst as the modern soother of the soul (2). At different times and indifferent societies, the dynamic between psychotherapy and religious authority may change, so that at times they seem to be at war with each other, and deny the validity of the other or claim they are destructive of societal values (3, 4), while at other times each may appreciate the role of the other and they may cooperate profitably (5). At first glance, there would seem to be intrinsic differences in their roles. A psychotherapist helps the sufferer gain relief from his distress, while a religious authority is primarily a leading member of a religious group, who can provide answers to religious questions, and, in this way, is God's presence on earth. A religious authority, therefore, has a responsibility to the religious group but also represents God's power to heal the individual.

There is a place for cooperation between therapists and clergy in most areas of mental health work (5), yet in few areas is the connection more interwoven than in religious symptoms in obsessive compulsive disorder (OCD). OCD is a common mental health problem found in all societies (6). The first descriptions of the condition were of religious symptoms: blasphemous thoughts and repetitive religious rituals, such as Luther's protracted confessions (7). Freud saw a clear parallel, both behavioral and in the underlying emotions, between religious rituals and compulsive behaviors (8). The typical cognitive processes that are associated with OCD have been noted as inflated responsibility, the importance ascribed to thoughts and their control, overestimation of threat, intolerance of uncertainty and perfectionism, and Rachman has noted that such features are associated with religious belief and instruction (9). Although there are claims that OCD is more common among the religious (10), there are also counter-claims (11) and OCD is common in all societies, religious and secular groups.

Religious symptoms are commonly found in OCD, and range from 5% to 50% of sufferers in a range of studies (11). In our studies in the ultra-orthodox Jewish community, for whom religious study and practice are central features of their lives, 39 out of 47 (83%) of our referrals diagnosed with OCD had religious symptoms (12, 13). The religious content of symptoms of OCD that typically appear in this population are clearly based on religious ritual (prayer, cleanliness before prayer, menstrual purity and dietary laws) and yet the form is characteristic of OCD in all cultures (repetitive thoughts, washing, checking, repeating) (12).

Members of the ultra-orthodox Jewish community turn to their religious authorities (rabbi, hassidic *rebbe*, *rosh yeshiva*) with questions concerning religious practice and also seek their guidance and support in coping with illness, and even choice of business ventures and spouse. Studies in the US have found that over 40% of referrals to a mental health center have sought spiritual help beforehand (14). In the case of religious symptoms of OCD among ultra-orthodox Jews, the patients maintain that their compulsive behaviors are performed according to the dictates of the codes of Jewish law, so that they initially believe that they are fulfilling religious law and only after some time realize that they are suffering and not functioning as they had previously. On both counts, for advice on matters of religious law and for help with their distress, the first place they turn for help is their rabbi (13).

A US authority on OCD, Baer, has written: "Jews with religious obsessions might try to talk to a Reform Rabbi, since an Orthodox Rabbi who was unfamiliar with obsessions could unknowingly reinforce an obsessional fear" (15, p.111). For an ultra-orthodox Jew, seeking counsel from a Reform rabbi is unthinkable as the basic tenets of Reform Judaism and its attitude to the sanctity of the laws are different from those of orthodox Judaism. Such counsel from a therapist challenges the worldview of most orthodox and all ultra-orthodox patients (for discussions of the distinctions between secular, conservative, reform, traditional, orthodox and ultra-orthodox, see 16). Is Baer correct, however, in his prediction of the response of ultra-orthodox rabbis to religious symptoms of OCD, that out of respect for Jewish ritual and ignorance of psychopathology they will opt for defense of the faith? Will the patient be told his meticulousness is meritorious and he should continue to pray with such devotion? In this study, the writing of two leading rabbis and the accounts of patients will be presented in order to evaluate the approach of these rabbis in the ultra-orthodox community to religious symptoms of OCD, what are its components, and how it compares and whether it can be incorporated into current treatments for OCD.

Religious OCD in Early Jewish Sources

In general, Jewish law is a set of injunctions, with emphasis on precision and care. By its very definition, a code of law will not provide examples of leniency towards elements of religious practice. Nevertheless, one unusual example of such apparent leniency will be presented. A common presentation of religious OCD is repeated housecleaning before the festival of Passover, when one is meant to ensure there is no bread in the home. The second century Mishna states: "[When cleaning the bread out of one's house on Passover eve] One should not fear that a weasel may have dragged [a breadcrumb] from one house [not yet cleaned] to another house [already cleaned], or from one place to another place. For in that case why not from one courtyard to another, or from one city to another — and there would be no end to the matter!" (Mishna Pesachim, 1:2). While discussing the law that bread should be neither seen nor found during Passover, the Mishna brings a question in order to define what can be expected of people, and whether the possibility of something untoward occurring need be considered. The Mishna may be seen to be engaging in a legal/philosophical discussion on the nature of certainty. However, on a concrete level, it may be seen to be demonstrating an awareness that some may take the need to be "bread-free" to extremes as "something may happen," and the author of the Mishna sees no virtue in this extreme.

Religious OCD in Recent Rabbinic Responsa

The written texts are the setting of religious boundaries or the community, as in texts of jurisprudence, so that one would neither expect them to be a source of statements of leniency, although these are not uncommon, nor a guide to the management of disorders of the individual members. Nevertheless, in each generation leaders emerge with a particular interest in mental suffering. They have religious stature that empowers them to prescribe for individuals who seek their help, and when the question is one of general interest, the written reply of the rabbi, known as a responsum, may be published and used for others who find themselves in similar difficulties.

Rabbi Yaacov Yisrael Kanievski (1899–1985) was known for his guidance on mental health issues, and had a particular expertise in religious OCD. He would receive questions and write his advice in letter form, and after his death these questions and responsa were gathered under various topics, with a section devoted to mental health issues. The following responsum relates to repetition in prayer, the commonest religious symptom found in ultra-orthodox Jewish men:

"Question: An important young man is unable to concentrate when he reads the *Shema*, and repeats each word many times, so as to pronounce each word properly and with exactness, and also out of concern that he did not have the correct concentration on the meaning of the words. And he is in doubt if he had the correct intention of fulfilling the commandment of saying the *Shema* properly. All of which causes the saying of the *Shema* to cause him great tension and takes a lot of time."

Rabbi Kanievski's reply: "It is my custom in these cases to tell him that he need only say the words in the prayer book. Even if it seems to him that he has not concentrated, he should continue further [and not repeat] (for deep inside he knows what he has said if he understands Hebrew, and even if he does not understand Hebrew, nevertheless his reading is an act of accepting the yoke of the kingdom of heaven). In this way he has fulfilled his duty of saying the *Shema*. It is forbidden to give him reasons or explanations, for every reason that he is given, he will undermine to contradict and reject completely whatever he was told. When he appears undecided he should be told decisively without any reasons at all. And after all these tricks, one needs a lot of help from Heaven, and may God have mercy on him and send him a complete recovery". (17, p. 45). This responsum has several fascinating aspects. The Code of Jewish Law, written by Rabbi Joseph Karo in the sixteenth century, is accepted in the orthodox Jewish world today as the definitive statement on Jewish law. It declares that the *Shema* be said with "devotion, awe, fear, shaking and trembling."

It is clear that Rabbi Kanievski recognizes the existence of a particular psychological disorder and the demands of the law are set aside. Further, he recognizes that the condition cannot be dealt with by a simple statement of guidance. He emphasizes twice that the sufferer must be given no explanation for the rabbi's decisions, as he will use such reasons in order to reject the directions he has received. This rejection of the advice of the rabbi would ordinarily be seen as a lack of respect for the authority of religion. In our experience from working with patients with OCD, repetitive requests for reassurance are common symptoms (e.g., Am I clean? Have I said that blessing properly?) (18). However, if a reassuring reply is offered to the OCD sufferer (e.g., You are definitely clean. I am sure you said the blessing properly), its effect is usually transient, either because the person is assailed by further thoughts or finds some rationale for rejecting the response, and so a new request for reassurance is made (19). In these details, it is clear that Rabbi Kanievski was experiencing the intrinsic difficulties of working with sufferers from OCD.

This aspect of the management is examined by Grinwald, the compiler of Rabbi Kanievski's responsa as follows: "If a person [with these obsessional concerns] goes and asks the opinion of a teacher of the law, the reply given will not calm him, since he will continue to have many doubts, that the authority asked did not hear properly, or did not understand his question sufficiently, or, even if he did hear, did not understand this specific picture in its details since he himself had not explained it adequately, etc., and there is no end to these doubts. And therefore, in order to avoid the fear of doubt, he is stringent with himself, and repeats the act again, and so it continues, God forbid, every time getting harder and more distressing" (17, p. 84). He continues: "There is no other advice than that he should teach himself to know and to believe with clarity that this is not the way of the holy Torah, whose "ways are pleasant ways" (Proverbs 3:17), and the Torah restores the soul of man and brings him pleasure and joy of the soul, as it says on joy in the Ways of the Righteous: Whoever carries out a commandment out of joy has one thousand times the reward of someone for whom the commandments area burden. "Ordinarily, a person may occasionally find himself in a situation where it is difficult to carry out a commandment so that he cannot perform it with the usual appropriate pleasure, for this is the nature of man. He sees this as a challenge and on the next occasion will carry it out with pleasure, since he usually performs commandments with enthusiasm and pleasure. However, the person who, whenever he performs the will of the Creator, finds his soul and his energies contorted by feelings of discomfort, fear, tension and misery over the carrying out of the commandment— and, on the contrary, this is his usual state, and to carry out commandments out of joy is the exception — this then is clear proof that this was not God's intention. For "strength and joy are in His place" (Chronicles I 16:27), meaning that the essence of performing commandments is joy, as Maimonides wrote (Mishne Tora, Laws of Lulav, 5:15): "The joy a person experiences in performing a commandment, and the love experienced for the most minor of them, is a great act of service, etc., and there is no greatness and honor but in rejoicing before God" (17, p. 85).

This discussion is particularly interesting in that the criterion used to differentiate between increased religiousness and religious OCD is absence of joy, or distress in OCD, consistent with the diagnosis in the international diagnostic manuals. The two commonest religious symptoms we have found among ultra-orthodox Jewish women are repetitive checking and washing concerning the separation of milk and meat according to the dietary laws, and checking and washing in the observation of the laws for menstrual purity (12). In some cases of the latter, it is the husband who is the patient.

Rabbi Kanievski received the following question: "A very important young husband has great difficulties over the [menstrual] purity of his wife, so that during the seven days of cleanliness [that are counted between the last signs of menstruation and going to the ritual bath prior to intercourse] he is full of fears and has endless doubts about every check [carried out by his wife during the seven days] and every speck [that might be blood or something else] over all these matters he practices great stringency so that he and his wife are very tense, and the entire household suffers very much." Rabbi Kanievski replied: "The only advice for this is that he [the husband] should not interfere in any way in the whole matter, for the Merciful one commanded the woman, as it is written: And **she** should count [not he, she], and all her questions and doubts she should take to a rabbi to ask (it is customary to ask the rabbi's wife who will ask the rabbi) and he must know that he has no right at all to have any stringencies, as it explains in the Talmud Nidda 12 that it is forbidden to be more strict than is necessary, since it would result in remorse and separation and would prevent fulfillment of 'be fruitful and multiply' [the commandment of procreation], and the commandment of conjugal rights. The rule in such situations is as it says: do not be too righteous, for by law a wife is trusted by her husband in such matters, and he should not interfere in any way to look at her showings and her checks [for menstrual bleeding]. Instead the wife should arrange it all, and when she has doubts she should ask a rabbi (accepted by them both as an authority), and with God's help his nerves should slowly settle on this matter. "And where it says: Do not be too righteous, the simple meaning is that righteousness of this kind can lead to madness, God forbid, and this will result in his not fulfilling all 613 commandments...." (17, p. 60). This particular example is interesting in that the solution is to take the problem out of his territory and authority. Such a tactic sees the problem as isolated, not related to a more general problem, and also may be seen as "relieving" him of responsibility. Can this be therapeutic, or is it likely to be of transient benefit like reassurance-seeking?

Another religious symptom of OCD that is common among ultra-orthodox Jewish males is repetitive washing of the peri-anal area before thrice-daily prayers. This will be used as an opportunity to demonstrate the dynamic relationship between the apparently rigid code of law quoted by patients to justify their compulsive behaviors and the response of rabbis. The Code of Jewish Law states: "If a person needs to go to the toilet, he should not pray, and if he did pray, then his prayer is an abomination and he should repeat his prayers. This is the case if he cannot wait for the time it takes to walk a 'parsa' (a parasang, about 4 kilometers), but if he can delay going to the bathroom for such a period of time, then in retrospect his prayers were acceptable [and need not be repeated]. But in the first place, a person should not pray until he has examined himself properly" (Code of Jewish Law, Orakh Hayyim, 92:1). The above should be contrasted with the next two written statements, remarkable for their explicit recognition of religious OCD.

"Question: A young man who has doubts in the synagogue if he cleaned himself properly or whether some [feces] were left, in which case he is unfit to pray or study or learn Torah, and he is very disturbed by this, cleans himself excessively, but his mind is not settled, and he is consumed by his doubts as to whether he is permitted to perform any acts of holiness [prayer or study]."

Rabbi Kanievsky replies: "In the matter of cleanliness [before prayer] I was very lenient according to the responsa of the Divrei Haim of Zanz [Rabbi Hayyim Halberstam, 1793–1876, founder of the Hassidic Zanz dynasty], who wrote that since in the time of the Talmud, they would only use three stones[to clean themselves perianally] and this was considered adequate, I settled that one can use five or six sheets of toilet paper and then rinse the area with a little water, as the rabbis wrote, basing themselves on the Ari [Isaac Luria, sixteenth century mystic]. After this, one should not check if one is clean or not, apart from wiping away the water, for if moisture is left it can cause sores. The principle is: after a brief rinse and wash, one should no longer check if anything remains and one can rely on Divrei Hayyim's opinion [that this is adequate].

"On several occasions young men have come to me suffering terribly with this problem.... And I know of some young men (now no longer young but in their middle age) whom I really saved from disintegration with this [approach] while one was very stubborn, and always thought he was in the right remained in a state in which he does not pray at all, God forbid, and he is in a very sick state" (17, p. 53).

Rabbi Kanievski's statement is again intriguing in that he takes the strict law and writes that in cases of OCD, where the written law has been the foundation for excessive cleaning, he has put his authority behind a definition limiting the number of toilet papers to be used, so that, even if the sufferer still feels unclean, he must not continue.

Further, arising out of his many years of experience he provides his readers with long-term follow-up: he has seen many men for whom his guidance was crucial to enable them to function, while another, who would not accept Rabbi Kanievski's authority, continued to suffer throughout his life.

This same problem of excessive cleaning before prayer was discussed by another historic hassidic leader, Rabbi Nahman of Bratslav (1772–1810) (20). What is particularly arresting is that his advice was given two hundred years ago. Rabbi Nahman's writings have reached enlarging new audiences today, and the reasons for this are apparent in this document, striking for its blunt wisdom, a "multidisciplinary" approach, and his identification with the sufferer: "Concerning those people who spend a lot of time on [perianal] cleanliness and spend a long time in the toilet [Rabbi Nahman was both very severe and scornful, and he dwelt at length on this matter. The main principle is that the Torah was not given to the ministering angels, and there is no need to be stricter than the law itself. According to the law, it is forbidden [to pray] only when one definitely needs to go to the toilet, as it states in the Talmud: One who needs to go the toilet should not pray; it is specifically referring to one who actually has a need. Even if one actually needs to go to the toilet there are laws about extenuating circumstances as brought in the Code of Jewish Law 92, who permit [prayer] *ab initio* if the person can delay for a distance of a parasang. From this we learn that if he does not actually need to go, there is no need to be strict and to waste time that would be spent in Torah study and prayer, because of anxieties, excessive strictness, and plain madness. "Instead, it is the right thing to pray in the morning first thing after getting out of bed. If it is possible to briefly go to the toilet that is fine, but if not, then not, and rather pray immediately. Even if he has a stomach ache, he should pay no attention and ignore it completely.

"In addition it is unnecessary to spend a long time in the toilet for it is very harmful to one's physical health and causes various ailments, particularly in our toilets in which the [anal] contents hang down, and this hanging is very, very injurious, causing the well-known disorder of hemorrhoids, may God have mercy. For this reason one should be very careful not to spend too long in the toilet, and one should not look for strictness and melancholy in this matter, for [such a form of strictness] was never discussed in the earlier generations. Rabbi Nahman had himself made this error earlier in his life and would do very strange things to achieve [peri-anal] cleanliness, and as a result nearly endangered his health and was not spared ailments as a consequence. Now he understands and says that it is all madness and, God forbid, one must not waste precious time on it. Further it is truly impossible to achieve a completely clean body without anything [unclean], for even if one was to fast from one Sabbath to the next, one would still need to go to the toilet at the end of the week, despite having eaten nothing for days. For something is always left in the body. "And Rabbi Nahman said it was a very important matter for him to have spoken on this subject for a very important conclusion emerges: that one should not spend a long time on this [matter] and not spend a long time there [in the toilet]. Even if occasionally one must take longer, better to go out and return rather than stay there for an extended time." (Sihot HaRan, 30).

This document is remarkable for its psychological sophistication. Rabbi Nahman is well aware of the existence of this problem, a form of OCD. He attacks from a series of vantage points: first showing that it is an incorrect understanding of the law, then explaining that it interferes with the most important values of prayer and Torah study, and then dealing with the little tricks that ensnare a person with OCD, the worrying tummy ache, the occasional need to spend longer that can restart the problem unless the person is wary. He argues that such practices cause physical illnesses and, presumably based on his own experiences of ascetic practices such as eating only on the Sabbath, he undertakes a cognitive-style approach that having a completely clean body is impossible to achieve. Finally, having berated the sufferers as mad, melancholic and overly scrupulous he confesses that he himself suffered from the disorder.

A further example will be brought of the law and its interpretation in the presence of compulsive behavior. The laws of cleaning for Passover are indeed stringent about clearing one's property of the presence of bread before the festival. The Code of Jewish Law states: "Some are accustomed to scrape the walls and chairs that were touched by leavened bread, and they have a basis for such action." The Mishnah Berurah, an authoritative and relatively recent commentary by Israel Meir Ha-Kohen (1838–1933) adds: "This means that one should not scoff at the custom and say it is foolish and excessively stringent" (Orakh Hayyim 442:6). Nevertheless: "Also in the matter of excessive stringency on Passover Rabbi Nahman of Bratslav did not agree at all with those who are too punctilious and enter into deep melancholy. He dwelt in detail on this matter, for one of our people [his followers] asked him a single question about how to behave concerning a particular stringency on Passover. And Rabbi Nahman was very scornful of him and spoke at length that it is unnecessary to look for excessive stringencies and madness and confusions. He said that he himself had also been very consumed by this matter that very excessive stringencies would occur to him. On one occasion he found himself thinking about the matter of water on Passover. He became anxious that perhaps the water that had been drawn could have leavened bread in it. He decided that he could prepare water for himself for the entire Passover holiday [eight days], but this too was not acceptable for it would be difficult to guard the water [from contact with bread] from Passover eve throughout all the days of the festival, until he realized that the only answer was flowing spring water that was flowing with fresh water at all times. However there was no such spring where he was living, so he was considering traveling to a place where there was such a spring... Just so far had he gone with stringencies, melancholy and excessive punctiliousness. But now he scoffs at it for it is unnecessary to look for excessive stringencies even on Passover". (Sihot HaRan, 235).

Excessive stringency, confusion, melancholy and madness are the terms used by Rabbi Nahman for his own behavior over the laws of Passover over two hundred years ago, realizing that some may carry the laws to excess. Rabbi Nahman's anecdote of his own experiences demonstrates that once punctilious observance begins to cause suffering in the person and their family there must be room for leniency. Reflecting an awareness of the size of the problem and the need for a special response, a pamphlet was produced a few years ago in Jerusalem on the subject of *"nerven"* (Yiddish for nerves), a term used by the ultra-orthodox community to refer to the religious symptoms of OCD. The pamphlet, called *Yir'ah tehora* (Hebrew: pure awe) has a note of endorsement from the son of Rabbi Kanievski on the front cover that he has read the contents, agrees with it and has encouraged that it be published. Of interest, the pamphlet discusses problems of male sufferers alone. The pamphlet is divided into two sections, the first for those in the early stages of *"nerven,"* and the second for those with the condition well-established. The first part takes the main religious symptoms of OCD that have been discussed here and elsewhere (12) and presents the written sources in order to prove that the sufferers have erred in their judgment, and that what they are doing is not in fulfillment of Jewish law. For example, while patients who are concerned that they will not say the *Shema* with devotion often pause or even freeze as they are about to say it in order to heighten their devotion, he shows that this is against the demands of Law, and that one *must not* pause. Aware that there is a debate whether prayers must be said with devotion, he brings a minimal definition of devotion that implies one need not concentrate on the words said. Concerning those who repeat words because they fear they did not say them correctly, whose position is apparently supported by an entire chapter in the Code of Jewish Law (Orakh

Hayim, 61) that brings examples of ends of words that need to be separated carefully from the next word, he brings the statement that if one was drowsy throughout the prayer, one should not go back and repeat (ibid., 63:5), as a proof that the prayer of the regular pray-er is acceptable and requires neither checking nor repetition. Concerning the symptom of checking whether *tefilin* (phylacteries) are properly placed on the forehead, he quotes the Divrei Haim that such behavior is "foolishness," for wherever it is placed on the forehead is satisfactory. On the subject of peri-anal cleaning, the author is more coy, sending the reader to more detailed sources. In summarizing the general attitude to prayer, the author states: "if when he is praying individually it is not possible to pray at the normal pace of respected leaders of prayer, then it is clear that he is erring in all his ways, in which case he is also casting aspersions and insult on all the holy people and on all our rabbis...." (21, p. 13).

The second briefer section concerns established cases of "*nerven,*" where the problem has become "second nature" and the appeals to study and thought no longer help. In such cases the sufferer must "declare war to the bitter end, a holy war!" He goes on to quote leading rabbis that in such cases the "clear ruling" is that they are exempt from all prayer until they return to the usual pleasurable form of prayer. The author repeats Rabbi Kanievski's advice that they should be given no rationale for this and other decisions in this situation, as otherwise "they will seek all sorts of useless reasons to contradict the truth of rabbinic opinion (Hebrew: daat Torah) and claim all sorts of absurdities and foolish and empty reasons, and all in order to continue their bad habits" (21, p.19).

Verbal Advice from Rabbis

The majority of advice given concerning religious OCD within the religious community occurs in a personal meeting between the sufferer or their representative (spouse or parent) and their rabbi, with no written record. This format makes it clear that the advice given is individually tailored and not to be seen as a general rule. It is our custom to ask our patient with religious OCD who is his rabbi. We have often given them letters of explanation for their rabbis so that the therapy can be authorized (16), and on a few occasions we have accompanied patients on a visit to their rabbi.

A woman was very concerned that she found signs of the cross wherever she walked, in the pavement, the window frames, etc., and that as a religious Jewish person she should avoid these signs of Christianity. She went to see her rabbi, renowned for his saintliness and understanding of mental health issues, and described her difficulties. In response, as she sat before him, he put one index finger across the other to form the shape of a cross, raised it to his lips and kissed the shape. His non-verbal response was to make it clear that there is a distinction between a religious symbol and everyday objects, and she was not to seek such symbols where they did not exist. His message was made even more powerful, as he was modeling "kissing the cross" to show that such everyday objects need cause no alarm and should be confronted.

A young man had approached his rabbi about his repetitions in prayer. His rituals of repetition concerned the most important section of the daily prayers, the *Shema*. His rabbi's reply was that he was to stop saying all three paragraphs of the *Shema* completely for two weeks. He returned to the rabbi after two weeks, and was now told to restore the third paragraph alone, with no repetitions. He returned two weeks later and the second paragraph was restored, the next visit all was restored except the first and most important sentence, the *Shema*. Finally, he was told to restore the *Shema* but to be careful not to repeat any parts of the prayer. For eight weeks this young man had left out the most important line of his daily prayers.

Discussion

Are the rabbis quoted above giving helpful advice to their followers with OCD or are they primarily defenders of the faith? As we have seen in the clinical examples, religious symptoms of OCD in ultra-orthodox Jewish patients occur in the normative setting of these laws: A person upset by his blasphemous thoughts will repeat the *Shema* because the codes define it as the most awesome moment of the daily prayer. A person who cleans to excess before Passover or spends hours cleaning himself before prayer will generally find support for his actions in the Code. However, once an individual begins to suffer from these behaviors that would hitherto have been praiseworthy signs of righteousness, and seeks guidance, all of the sources and rabbis that we have quoted present a very lenient attitude toward the practice of the laws in order to help find relief from suffering for people with OCD. On an individual basis and with the authority of the rabbi, the laws are contravened and repetitions banned.

The role of the rabbi differs from that of a therapist in several ways. The rabbi is an expert in Jewish law and has the authority to make decisions on religious matters. The therapist, on the other hand, is an expert on OCD. He may have status but not authority over the patient, whom he advises. This distinction is captured in the blessing we are often given by our ultra-orthodox patients: "May you be a good messenger [of God's will]." The therapist is a conduit of God's will, but not one with authority. If he gives advice, it is the rabbi who confirms whether it should be carried out. This distinction between therapist and authority is particularly striking in the writings of Rabbi Nahman of Bratslav, Rabbi Kanievski and the books based on his rulings, as they discussed the laws in the Jewish codes and redrew the limits of religious behavior for these individuals. The motivation was to alleviate the suffering and enable the person to pray well in the future at the expense of current religious duties. The authority to give such a pronouncement is clearly not the province of a mental health worker. Indeed, the case of stopping saying the *Shema* was recounted to one of us by the rabbi himself. Intrigued by the proximity of the approach to exposure in behavior therapy, the therapist responded: "I can't say that to my patients." "Correct," replied the rabbi. Are such interventions that are founded on authority effective therapy? In the early days of exposure treatment, compulsive hand-washers were hospitalized, the water supply to the ward was restricted, and the staff often guarded the patients physically to prevent them carrying out the compulsive behaviors (22). Such actions are now considered both unethical and ineffective. Treatment can only be undertaken with full consent, and the patient who is coerced is most likely to relapse once released from care. Is the use of rabbinic authority a form of coercion? The repeated warnings and admission of failure in some cases by Rabbi Kanievski suggest that however eminent the rabbi, it is not possible to effectively coerce a patient with religious OCD. The dialectic between the expectations and suffering of a client and the authority and expertise of a healer may be quite similar, whether the healer is a rabbi or a mental health worker (1).

The most effective intervention in OCD other than medication is the form of cognitive behavior therapy known as exposure and response prevention (ERP) (23). How does the intervention suggested by the rabbis compare with the principles of ERP? In ERP, the sufferer is asked to undertake activities that evoke the fears he is concerned with, while not carrying out the repetitive behaviors. Applying this to religious OCD, in the case of pre-Passover cleaning, the patient would be asked to clean once for a reasonable period of time, and then not repeat the cleaning. In the case of the *Shema*, the prayer would be said only once whether the sufferer thought he had said it correctly or not. In both statements there is consistency between the religious authorities quoted and cognitive-behavioral therapy.

Is the role of rabbinic authority one of giving reassurance that the sufferer from religious OCD has not sinned, thereby actually relieving him of individual responsibility? If so, its beneficial effects would be expected to be only transitory. Practically, the distinction between these two approaches appears minor: Rabbi Kanievski instructs to say the *Shema* but once, and the precept will have been fulfilled, whatever the person thinks. The cognitive-behavior therapist will ask to say the *Shema* once even if the person thinks he did not have proper concentration. The advice of all the religious authorities quoted here does not seem to be reinforcing the OCD behaviors, as Baer warned. On the other hand, does the therapist have the right to make such a suggestion to an ultra-orthodox patient unless he has the backing of an authority such as Rabbi Kanievski? Cooperation between priest and therapist in religious OCD was suggested by Minichiello, a priest and therapist, who considered that his Catholic patients with OCD have "a totally untheological view of God" (15, p. 107) and suggested that they discuss this with their priest before attempting ERT, and Ciarrocchi found that patients with religious OCD often refuse to embark on therapy and suggested a series of maneuvers of cooperation with the priest (15).

Finally, a dispute in the sixth century Talmud implies that the patient with repetitive religious behavior may have a problem in his relationship with God. In a discussion concerning the repetition of the *Shema*: "Rabbi Pappa said to Abaye: But perhaps the first time he said the verse he didn't have proper devotion, and the last time round he did? Abaye answered him: Is [his prayer] some type of friendly chat with Heaven? If he prayed without devotion from the outset, he should be beaten with a blacksmith's sledge hammer until he prays with devotion!" (Babylonian Talmud Brachot, 33:2–34:1)

The examples brought in this paper should be viewed with caution for several reasons: this was not a systematic study, asking all OCD sufferers to describe the responses of all rabbis they had approached with these symptoms, and while the two rabbis whose writings are presented are highly respected figures, there may be other responsa of which we are unaware. Further, as clinicians in a community mental health center, our sample of patients is inevitably those who have long-term difficulties, and had not been helped by advice only from their rabbi.

None of the rabbis consulted in these published accounts considered the possible role of a form of therapy beyond their own ability to help. This may be understood as similar to the contrast between the stringency found in religious texts and the flexibility in rabbi-sufferer interactions; so too, publicly the leaders of the ultra-orthodox Jewish community remain cautious in recommending psychotherapy. On an individual basis, however, they often keep abreast of developments in the field of mental health and are willing to recommend that their followers seek help, including in the area of religious OCD.

References

1. Frank JD. Persuasion and healing: A comparative study of psychotherapy. New York: Schocken, 1963.
2. Fromm E. Psychoanalysis and religion. New Haven: Yale University, 1967.
3. Amsel A. Judaism and psychology. New York: Feldheim, 1969.
4. Freud S. The future of an illusion. In: Standard Edition 21 (1927), trans. J Strachey. London: Hogarth, 1961:pp. 1–56.
5. Foskett J, Marriott J, Wilson-Rudd F. Mental health, religion and spirituality: Attitudes, experience and expertise among mental health professionals and religious leaders in Somerset. Ment Health Religion Culture 2004;7:5–22.

6. Weissman MM, Bland RG, Canino GJ, Greenwald S, Hwu H-G, Lee CK, Newman SC, Oakley-Browne MA, Rubio-Stipec M, Wickramaratne PJ, Wittchen H-U, Yeh E-Y (Cross National Collaborative Group): The cross-national epidemiology of obsessive-compulsive disorder. J Clin Psychiatry 1994; 55: 5–10.

7. Greenberg D, Witztum E, Pisante J. Scrupulosity: Religious attitudes and clinical presentations. Brit J Med Psychology 1987; 60: 29–37.

8. Freud S. Obsessive acts and religious practices In: Standard Edition 9 (1907), trans. J Strachey. London: Hogarth, 1959: pp. 115–127.

9. Rachman S. A cognitive theory of obsessions. Behav Res Ther 1997; 35:793–802.

10. Abramowitz JS, Deacon BJ, Woods CM, Tolin DF. Association between Protestant religiosity and obsessive-compulsive symptoms and cognitions. Depress Anxiety, 2004; 20: 70–76.

11. Tek C, Ulug B. Religiosity and religious obsessions on obsessive-compulsive disorder. Psychiatry Res 2001; 104: 99–108.

12. Greenberg D, Witztum E. The influence of cultural factors on obsessive compulsive disorder: Religious symptoms in a religious society. Isr J Psychiatry Relat Sci 1994; 31:211–220.

13. Greenberg D, Shefler G. Obsessive compulsive disorder in ultra-orthodox Jewish patients: A comparison of religious and non-religious symptoms. Psychol Psychother: Theory Res Practice 2002; 75:123–130.

14. Beitman BD. Pastoral counseling centers: A challenge to community mental health centers.Hosp CommPsychiatry 1982; 33:486–487.

15. Baer L. The imp of the mind: Exploring the silent epidemic of obsessive bad thoughts. New York: Plume, 2002.

16. Greenberg D, Witztum E. Sanity and sanctity: Mental health work among the ultra-orthodox in Jerusalem. New Haven: Yale University, 2001.

17. Grinwald JM. Advice and guidance based on the letters the rabbi "Kehillat Yaaacov" (Etzot vehadrachot), 5751 (1991) (Hebrew).

18. Morillo C, Belloch A, Garcia-Soriano G. Clinical obsessions in obsessive-compulsive patients and obsession-relevant intrusive thoughts in non-clinical, depressed and anxious subjects: Where are the differences? Behav Res Ther 2007; 45:1319–1333.

19. Renshaw KD, Steketee G, Chambless DL. Involving family members in the treatment of OCD. Cogn Behav Ther 2005;34:164–175.

20. Green A. Tormentedmaster: A life of RabbiNahman of Bratslav. New York: Schocken, 1981.

21. Pure awe (Yir'ah tehora). Jerusalem: Foundation for the advancement of Torah study, no date. (Hebrew).

22. Meyer V. Modification of expectations in cases with obsessional rituals. Behav Res Ther 1966; 4: 273–280.

23. Fisher PL, Wells A. How effective are cognitive and behavioral treatments for obsessive-compulsive disorder? Behav Res Ther 2005 ;43:1543–1558.

Acknowledgements

The author thanks Hava Ben Shalom, co-author of the first article and Brurit Laub, cotherapist and co-author of the fifth article for their contributions, Gefen Publishers for permission to reprint the last article that was originally published in the Israel Journal of Psychiatry and Related Sciences, vol. 45, No. 3 (2008), 183-192, Betty Hoffman for proofreading the manuscript and Dr. Richard and Marcia (Rothstein) Kashnow for their support in publishing the four publications of Nefesh Israel and advancing mental health education in Israel, especially in the dati/haredi community.

www.ingramcontent.com/pod-product-compliance
Lightning Source LLC
Chambersburg PA
CBHW020805160426
43192CB00006B/453